6. Enter your class ID code to joi

IF YOU HAVE A CLASS CODE FROM YOUR TEACHER

a. Enter your class code and click | **Next** |

b. Once you have joined a class, you will be able to use the Discussion Board and Email tools.

c. To enter this code later, choose **Join a Class**. 

IF YOU DO NOT HAVE A CLASS CODE

a. If you do not have a class ID code, click | **Skip** |

b. You do not need a class ID code to use *iQ Online*.

c. To enter this code later, choose **Join a Class**. 

7. Review registration information and click Log In. Then choose your book. Click **Activities** to begin using *iQ Online*. 

IMPORTANT

- After you register, the next time you want to use *iQ Online*, go to www.iQOnlinePractice.com and log in with your email address and password.
- The online content can be used for 12 months from the date you register.
- For help, please contact customer service: eltsupport@oup.com.

WHAT IS iQ ONLINE ?

All new activities provide essential skills **practice** and support.

Vocabulary and Grammar **games** immerse you in the language and provide even more practice.

Authentic, engaging **videos** generate new ideas and opinions on the Unit Question.

Go to the Media Center to download or stream all **student book audio**.

Use the **Discussion Board** to discuss the Unit Question and more.

Email encourages communication with your teacher and classmates.

Automatic grading gives immediate feedback and tracks progress.

Progress Reports show what you have mastered and where you still need more practice.

SHAPING *learning* TOGETHER

We would like to acknowledge the teachers from all over the world who participated in the development process and review of the Q series.

Special thanks to our *Q: Skills for Success* Second Edition Topic Advisory Board

Shaker Ali Al-Mohammad, Buraimi University College, Oman; **Dr. Asmaa A. Ebrahim**, University of Sharjah, U.A.E.; **Rachel Batchilder**, College of the North Atlantic, Qatar; **Anil Bayir**, Izmir University, Turkey; **Flora Mcvay Bozkurt**, Maltepe University, Turkey; **Paul Bradley**, University of the Thai Chamber of Commerce Bangkok, Thailand; **Joan Birrell-Bertrand**, University of Manitoba, MB, Canada; **Karen E. Caldwell**, Zayed University, U.A.E.; **Nicole Hammond Carrasquel**, University of Central Florida, FL, U.S.; **Kevin Countryman**, Seneca College of Applied Arts & Technology, ON, Canada; **Julie Crocker**, Arcadia University, NS, Canada; **Marc L. Cummings**, Jefferson Community and Technical College, KY, U.S.; **Rachel DeSanto**, Hillsborough Community College Dale Mabry Campus, FL, U.S.; **Nilüfer Ertürkmen**, Ege University, Turkey; **Sue Fine**, Ras Al Khaimah Women's College (HCT), U.A.E.; **Amina Al Hashami**, Nizwa College of Applied Sciences, Oman; **Stephan Johnson**, Nagoya Shoka Daigaku, Japan; **Sean Kim**, Avalon, South Korea; **Gregory King**, Chubu Daigaku, Japan; **Seran Küçük**, Maltepe University, Turkey; **Jonee De Leon**, VUS, Vietnam; **Carol Lowther**, Palomar College, CA, U.S.; **Erin Harris-MacLead**, St. Mary's University, NS, Canada; **Angela Nagy**, Maltepe University, Turkey; **Huynh Thi Ai Nguyen**, Vietnam; **Daniel L. Paller**, Kinjo Gakuin University, Japan; **Jangyo Parsons**, Kookmin University, South Korea; **Laila Al Qadhi**, Kuwait University, Kuwait; **Josh Rosenberger**, English Language Institute University of Montana, MT, U.S.; **Nancy Schoenfeld**, Kuwait University, Kuwait; **Jenay Seymour**, Hongik University, South Korea; **Moon-young Son**, South Korea; **Matthew Taylor**, Kinjo Gakuin Daigaku, Japan; **Burcu Tezcan-Unal**, Zayed University, U.A.E.; **Troy Tucker**, Edison State College-Lee Campus, FL, U.S.; **Kris Vicca**, Feng Chia University, Taichung; **Jisook Woo**, Incheon University, South Korea; **Dunya Yenidunya**, Ege University, Turkey

UNITED STATES **Marcarena Aguilar**, North Harris College, TX; **Rebecca Andrade**, California State University North Ridge, CA; **Lesley Andrews**, Boston University, MA; **Deborah Anholt**, Lewis and Clark College, OR; **Robert Anzelde**, Oakton Community College, IL; **Arlys Arnold**, University of Minnesota, MN; **Marcia Arthur**, Renton Technical College, WA; **Renee Ashmeade**, Passaic County Community College, NJ; **Anne Bachmann**, Clackamas Community College, OR; **Lida Baker**, UCLA, CA; **Ron Balsamo**, Santa Rosa Junior College, CA; **Lori Barkley**, Portland State University, OR; **Eileen Barlow**, SUNY Albany, NY; **Sue Bartch**, Cuyahoga Community College, OH; **Lora Bates**, Oakton High School, VA; **Barbara Batra**, Nassau County Community College, NY; **Nancy Baum**, University of Texas at Arlington, TX; **Rebecca Beck**, Irvine Valley College, CA; **Linda Berendsen**, Oakton Community College, IL; **Jennifer Binckes Lee**, Howard Community College, MD; **Grace Bishop**, Houston Community College, TX; **Jean W. Bodman**, Union County College, NJ; **Virginia Bouchard**, George Mason University, VA; **Kimberley Briesch Sumner**, University of Southern California, CA; **Kevin Brown**, University of California, Irvine, CA; **Laura Brown**, Glendale Community College, CA; **Britta Burton**, Mission College, CA; **Allison L. Callahan**, Harold Washington College, IL; **Gabriela Cambiasso**, Harold Washington College, IL; **Jackie Campbell**, Capistrano Unified School District, CA; **Adele C. Camus**, George Mason University, VA; **Laura Chason**, Savannah College, GA; **Kerry Linder Catana**, Language Studies International, NY; **An Cheng**, Oklahoma State University, OK; **Carole Collins**, North Hampton Community College, PA; **Betty R. Compton**, Intercultural Communications College, HI; **Pamela Couch**, Boston University, MA; **Fernanda Crowe**, Intrax International Institute, CA; **Vicki Curtis**, Santa Cruz, CA; **Margo Czinski**, Washtenaw Community College, MI; **David Dahnke**, Lone Star College, TX; **Gillian M. Dale**, CA; **L. Dalgish**, Concordia College, MN; **Christopher Davis**, John Jay College, NY; **Sherry Davis**, Irvine University, CA; **Natalia de Cuba**, Nassau County Community College, NY; **Sonia Delgadillo**, Sierra College, CA; **Esmeralda Diriye**, Cypress College & Cal Poly, CA; **Marta O. Dmytrenko-Ahrabian**, Wayne State University, MI; **Javier Dominguez**, Central High School, SC; **Jo Ellen Downey-Greer**, Lansing Community College, MI; **Jennifer Duclos**, Boston University, MA; **Yvonne Duncan**, City College of San Francisco, CA; **Paul Dydman**, USC Language Academy, CA; **Anna Eddy**, University of Michigan-Flint, MI; **Zohan El-Gamal**, Glendale Community College, CA; **Jennie Farnell**, University of Connecticut, CT; **Susan Fedors**, Howard Community College, MD; **Valerie Fiechter**, Mission College, CA; **Ashley Fifer**, Nassau County Community College, NY; **Matthew Florence**, Intrax International Institute, CA; **Kathleen Flynn**, Glendale College, CA; **Elizabeth Fonsea**, Nassau County Community College, NY; **Eve Fonseca**, St. Louis Community College, MO; **Elizabeth Foss**, Washtenaw Community College, MI; **Duff C. Galda**, Pima Community College, AZ; **Christiane Galvani**, Houston Community College, TX; **Gretchen Gerber**, Howard Community College, MD; **Ray Gonzalez**, Montgomery College, MD; **Janet Goodwin**, University of California, Los Angeles, CA; **Alyona Gorokhova**, Grossmont College, CA; **John Graney**, Santa Fe College, FL; **Kathleen Green**, Central High School, AZ; **Nancy Hamadou**, Pima Community College-West Campus, AZ; **Webb Hamilton**, De Anza College, San Jose City College, CA; **Janet Harclerode**, Santa Monica Community College, CA; **Sandra Hartmann**, Language and Culture Center, TX; **Kathy Haven**, Mission College, CA; **Roberta Hendrick**, Cuyahoga Community College, OH; **Ginny Heringer**, Pasadena City College, CA; **Adam Henricksen**, University of Maryland, MD; **Carolyn Ho**, Lone Star College-CyFair, TX; **Peter Hoffman**, LaGuardia Community College, NY; **Linda Holden**, College of Lake County, IL; **Jana Holt**, Lake Washington Technical College, WA; **Antonio Iccarino**, Boston University, MA; **Gail Ibele**, University of Wisconsin, WI; **Nina Ito**, American Language Institute, CSU Long Beach, CA; **Linda Jensen**, UCLA, CA; **Lisa Jurkowitz**, Pima Community College, CA; **Mandy Kama**, Georgetown University, Washington, DC; **Stephanie Kasuboski**, Cuyahoga Community College, OH; **Chigusa Katoku**, Mission College, CA; **Sandra Kawamura**, Sacramento City College, CA; **Gail Kellersberger**, University of Houston-Downtown, TX; **Jane Kelly**, Durham Technical Community College, NC; **Maryanne Kildare**, Nassau County Community College, NY; **Julie Park Kim**, George Mason University, VA; **Kindra Kinyon**, Los Angeles Trade-Technical College, CA; **Matt Kline**, El Camino College, CA; **Lisa Kovacs-Morgan**, University of California, San Diego, CA; **Claudia Kupiec**, DePaul University, IL; **Renee La Rue**, Lone Star College-Montgomery, TX; **Janet Langon**, Glendale College, CA; **Lawrence Lawson**, Palomar College, CA; **Rachele Lawton**, The Community College of Baltimore County, MD; **Alice Lee**, Richland College, TX; **Esther S. Lee**, CSUF & Mt. SAC, CA; **Cherie Lenz-Hackett**, University of Washington, WA; **Joy Leventhal**, Cuyahoga Community College, OH; **Alice Lin**, UCI Extension, CA; **Monica Lopez**, Cerritos College, CA; **Dustin Lovell**, FLS International Marymount College, CA; **Carol Lowther**, Palomar College, CA; **Candace Lynch-Thompson**, North Orange County Community College District, CA; **Thi Thi Ma**, City College of San Francisco, CA; **Steve Mac Isaac**, USC Long Academy, CA; **Denise Maduli-Williams**, City College of San Francisco, CA; **Eileen Mahoney**, Camelback High School, AZ; **Naomi Mardock**, MCC-Omaha, NE; **Brigitte Maronde**, Harold Washington College, IL; **Marilyn Marquis**, Laposita College CA; **Doris Martin**, Glendale Community College; Pasadena City College, CA; **Keith Maurice**, University of Texas at Arlington, TX; **Nancy Mayer**, University of Missouri-St. Louis, MO; **Aziah McNamara**, Kansas State University, KS; **Billie McQuillan**, Education Heights, MN; **Karen Merritt**, Glendale Union High School District, AZ; **Holly Milkowart**, Johnson County Community College, KS; **Eric Moyer**, Intrax International Institute, CA; **Gino Muzzatti**, Santa Rosa Junior College, CA; **Sandra Navarro**, Glendale Community College, CA; **Than Nyeinkhin**, ELAC, PCC, CA; **William Nedrow**, Triton College, IL; **Eric Nelson**, University of Minnesota, MN; **Than Nyeinkhin**, ELAC, PCC, CA; **Fernanda Ortiz**, Center for English as a Second Language at the University of Arizona, AZ; **Rhony Ory**, Ygnacio Valley High School, CA; **Paul Parent**, Montgomery College, MD; **Dr. Sumeeta Patnaik**, Marshall University, WV; **Oscar Pedroso**, Miami Dade College, FL; **Robin Persiani**, Sierra College, CA; **Patricia Prenz-Belkin**, Hostos Community College, NY; **Suzanne Powell**, University of Louisville, KY; **Jim Ranalli**, Iowa State University, IA; **Toni R. Randall**, Santa Monica College, CA; **Vidya Rangachari**, Mission College, CA; **Elizabeth Rasmussen**, Northern Virginia Community College, VA; **Lara Ravitch**, Truman College, IL;

Deborah Repasz, San Jacinto College, TX; Marisa Recinos, English Language Center, Brigham Young University, UT; Andrey Reznikov, Black Hills State University, SD; Alison Rice, Hunter College, NY; Jennifer Robles, Ventura Unified School District, CA; Priscilla Rocha, Clark County School District, NV; Dzidra Rodins, DePaul University, IL; Maria Rodriguez, Central High School, AZ; Josh Rosenberger, English Language Institute University of Montana, MT; Alice Rosso, Bucks County Community College, PA; Rita Rozzi, Xavier University, OH; Maria Ruiz, Victor Valley College, CA; Kimberly Russell, Clark College, WA; Stacy Sabraw, Michigan State University, MI; Irene Sakk, Northwestern University, IL; Deborah Sandstrom, University of Illinois at Chicago, IL; Jenni Santamaria, ABC Adult, CA; Shaeley Santiago, Ames High School, IA; Peg Sarosy, San Francisco State University, CA; Alice Savage, North Harris College, TX; Donna Schaeffer, University of Washington, WA; Karen Marsh Schaeffer, University of Utah, UT; Carol Schinger, Northern Virginia Community College, VA; Robert Scott, Kansas State University, KS; Suell Scott, Sheridan Technical Center, FL; Shira Seaman, Global English Academy, NY; Richard Seltzer, Glendale Community College, CA; Harlan Sexton, CUNY Queensborough Community College, NY; Kathy Sherak, San Francisco State University, CA; German Silva, Miami Dade College, FL; Ray Smith, Maryland English Institute, University of Maryland, MD; Shira Smith, NICE Program University of Hawaii, HI; Tara Smith, Felician College, NJ; Monica Snow, California State University, Fullerton, CA; Elaine Soffer, Nassau County Community College, NY; Andrea Spector, Santa Monica Community College, CA; Jacqueline Sport, LBWCC Luverne Center, AL; Karen Stanely, Central Piedmont Community College, NC; Susan Stern, Irvine Valley College, CA; Ayse Stromsdorfer, Soldan I.S.H.S., MO; Yilin Sun, South Seattle Community College, WA; Thomas Swietlik, Intrax International Institute, IL; Nicholas Taggert, University of Dayton, OH; Judith Tanka, UCLA Extension–American Language Center, CA; Amy Taylor, The University of Alabama Tuscaloosa, AL; Andrea Taylor, San Francisco State, CA; Priscilla Taylor, University of Southern California, CA; Ilene Teixeira, Fairfax County Public Schools, VA; Shirl H. Terrell, Collin College, TX; Marya Teutsch-Dwyer, St. Cloud State University, MN; Stephen Thergesen, ELS Language Centers, CO; Christine Tierney, Houston Community College, TX; Arlene Turini, North Moore High School, NC; Cara Tuzzolino, Nassau County Community College, NY; Suzanne Van Der Valk, Iowa State University, IA; Nathan D. Vasarhely, Ygnacio Valley High School, CA; Naomi S. Verratti, Howard Community College, MD; Hollyahna Vettori, Santa Rosa Junior College, CA; Julie Vorholt, Lewis & Clark College, OR; Danielle Wagner, FLS International Marymount College, CA; Lynn Walker, Coastline College, CA; Laura Walsh, City College of San Francisco, CA; Andrew J. Watson, The English Bakery; Donald Weasenforth, Collin College, TX; Juliane Widner, Sheepshead Bay High School, NY; Lynne Wilkins, Mills College, CA; Pamela Williams, Ventura College, CA; Jeff Wilson, Irvine Valley College, CA; James Wilson, Consomnes River College, CA; Katie Windahl, Cuyahoga Community College, OH; Dolores "Lorrie" Winter, California State University at Fullerton, CA; Jody Yamamoto, Kapi'olani Community College, HI; Ellen L. Yaniv, Boston University, MA; Norman Yoshida, Lewis & Clark College, OR; Joanna Zadra, American River College, CA; Florence Zysman, Santiago Canyon College, CA;

CANADA Patricia Birch, Brandon University, MB; Jolanta Caputa, College of New Caledonia, BC; Katherine Coburn, UBC's ELI, BC; Erin Harris-Macleod, St. Mary's University, NS; Tami Moffatt, English Language Institute, BC; Jim Papple, Brock University, ON; Robin Peace, Confederation College, BC;

ASIA Rabiatu Abubakar, Eton Language Centre, Malaysia; Wiwik Andreani, Bina Nusantara University, Indonesia; Frank Bailey, Baiko Gakuin University, Japan; Mike Baker, Kosei Junior High School, Japan; Leonard Barrow, Kanto Junior College, Japan; Herman Bartelen, Japan; Siren Betty, Fooyin University, Kaohsiung; Thomas E. Bieri, Nagoya College, Japan; Natalie Brezden, Global English House, Japan; MK Brooks, Mukogawa Women's University, Japan; Truong Ngoc Buu, The Youth Language School, Vietnam; Charles Cabell, Toyo University, Japan; Fred Carruth, Matsumoto University, Japan; Frances Causer, Seijo University, Japan; Jeffrey Chalk, SNU, South Korea; Deborah Chang, Wenzao Ursuline College of Languages, Kaohsiung; David Chatham, Ritsumeikan University, Japan; Andrew Chih Hong Chen, National Sun Yat-sen University, Kaohsiung; Christina Chen, Yu-Tsai Bilingual Elementary School, Taipei; Hui-chen Chen, Shi-Lin High School of Commerce, Taipei; Seungmoon Choe, K2M Language Institute, South Korea; Jason Jeffree Cole, Coto College, Japan; Le Minh Cong, Vungtau Tourism Vocational College, Vietnam; Todd Cooper, Toyama National College of Technology, Japan; Marie Cosgrove, Daito Bunka University, Japan; Randall Cotten, Gifu City Women's College, Japan; Tony Cripps, Ritsumeikan University, Japan; Andy Cubalit, CHS, Thailand; Daniel Cussen, Takushoku University, Japan; Le Dan, Ho Chi Minh City Electric Power College, Vietnam; Simon Daykin, Banghwa-dong Community Centre, South Korea; Aimee Denham, ILA, Vietnam; Bryan Dickson, David's English Center, Taipei; Nathan Ducker, Japan University, Japan; Ian Duncan, Simul International Corporate Training, Japan; Nguyen Thi Kieu Dung, Thang Long University, Vietnam; Truong Quang Dung, Tien Giang University, Vietnam; Nguyen Thi Thuy Duong, Vietnamese American Vocational Training College, Vietnam; Wong Tuck Ee, Raja Tun Azlan Science Secondary School, Malaysia; Emilia Effendy, International Islamic University Malaysia, Malaysia; Bettizza Escueta, KMUTT, Thailand; Robert Eva, Kaisei Girls High School, Japan; Jim George, Luna International Language School, Japan; Jurgen Germeys, Silk Road Language Center, South Korea; Wong Ai Gnoh, SMJK Chung Hwa Confucian, Malaysia; Sarah Go, Seoul Women's University, South Korea; Peter Goosselink, Hokkai High School, Japan; Robert Gorden, SNU, South Korea; Wendy M. Gough, St. Mary College/Nunoike Gaigo Senmon Gakko, Japan; Tim Grose, Sapporo Gakuin University, Japan; Pham Thu Ha, Le Van Tam Primary School, Vietnam; Ann-Marie Hadzima, Taipei; Troy Hammond, Tokyo Gakugei University International Secondary School, Japan; Robiatul 'Adawiah Binti Hamzah, SMK Putrajaya Precinct 8(1), Malaysia; Tran Thi Thuy Hang, Ho Chi Minh City Banking University, Vietnam; To Thi Hong Hanh, CEFALT, Vietnam; George Hays, Tokyo Kokusai Daigaku, Japan; Janis Hearn, Hongik University, South Korea; Chantel Hemmi, Jochi Daigaku, Japan; David Hindman, Sejong University, South Korea; Nahn Cam Hoa, Ho Chi Minh City University of Technology, Vietnam; Jana Holt, Korea University, South Korea; Jason Hollowell, Nihon University, Japan; F. N. (Zoe) Hsu, National Tainan University, Yong Kang; Kuei-ping Hsu, National Tsing Hua University, Hsinchu City; Wenhua Hsu, I-Shou University, Kaohsiung; Luu Nguyen Quoc Hung, Cantho University, Vietnam; Cecile Hwang, Changwon National University, South Korea; Ainol Haryati Ibrahim, Universiti Malaysia Pahang, Malaysia; Robert Jeens, Yonsei University, South Korea; Linda M. Joyce, Kyushu Sangyo University, Japan; Dr. Nisai Kaewsanchai, English Square Kanchanaburi, Thailand; Aniza Kamarulzaman, Sabah Science Secondary School, Malaysia; Ikuko Kashiwabara, Osaka Electro-Communication University, Japan; Gurmit Kaur, INTI College, Malaysia; Nick Keane, Japan; Ward Ketcheson, Aomori University, Japan; Nicholas Kemp, Kyushu International University, Japan; Montchatry Ketmuni, Rajamangala University of Technology, Thailand; Dinh Viet Khanh, Vietnam; Seonok Kim, Kangsu Jongro Language School, South Korea; Suyeon Kim, Anyang University, South Korea; Kelly P. Kimura, Soka University, Japan; Masakazu Kimura, Katoh Gakuen Gyoshu High School, Japan; Gregory King, Chubu Daigaku, Japan; Stan Kirk, Konan University, Japan; Donald Knight, Nan Hua/Fu Li Junior High Schools, Hsinchu; Kari J. Kostiainen, Nagoya City University, Japan; Pattri Kuanpulpol, Silpakorn University, Thailand; Ha Thi Lan, Thai Binh Teacher Training College, Vietnam; Eric Edwin Larson, Miyazaki Prefectural Nursing University, Japan; David Laurence, Chubu Daigaku, Japan; Richard S. Lavin, Prefectural University of Kumamoto, Japan; Shirley Leane, Chugoku Junior College, Japan; I-Hsiu Lee, Yunlin; Nari Lee, Park Jung PLS, South Korea; Tae Lee, Yonsei University, South Korea; Lys Yongsoon Lee, Reading Town Geumcheon, South Korea; Mallory Leece, Sun Moon University, South Korea; Dang Hong Lien, Tan Lam Upper Secondary School, Vietnam; Huang Li-Han, Rebecca Education Institute, Taipei; Sovannarith Lim, Royal University of Phnom Penh, Cambodia; Ginger Lin, National Kaohsiung Hospitality College, Kaohsiung; Noel Lineker, New Zealand/Japan; Tran Dang Khanh Linh, Nha Trang Teachers' Training College, Vietnam; Daphne Liu, Buliton English School, Taipei; S. F. Josephine Liu, Tien-Mu Elementary School, Taipei; Caroline Luo, Tunghai University, Taichung; Jeng-Jia Luo, Tunghai University, Taichung; Laura MacGregor, Gakushuin University, Japan; Amir Madani, Visuttharangsi School, Thailand; Elena Maeda, Sacred Heart Professional Training College, Japan; Vu Thi Thanh Mai, Hoang Gia Education Center, Vietnam; Kimura Masakazu, Kato Gakuen Gyoshu High School, Japan; Susumu Matsuhashi, Net Link English School, Japan; James McCrostie, Daito Bunka University, Japan; Joel McKee, Inha University, South Korea; Colin McKenzie, Wachirawit Primary School, Thailand; Terumi Miyazoe, Tokyo Denki Daigaku, Japan; William K. Moore, Hiroshima Kokusai Gakuin University, Japan; Kevin Mueller, Tokyo Kokusai Daigaku, Japan; Hudson Murrell, Baiko Gakuin University, Japan; Frances Namba, Senri International School of Kwansei Gakuin, Japan; Keiichi Narita, Niigata University, Japan; Kim Chung Nguyen, Ho Chi Minh University of

Industry, Vietnam; **Do Thi Thanh Nhan**, Hanoi University, Vietnam; **Dale Kazuo Nishi**, Aoyama English Conversation School, Japan; **Huynh Thi Ai Nguyen**, Vietnam; **Dongshin Oh**, YBM PLS, South Korea; **Keiko Okada**, Dokkyo Daigaku, Japan; **Louise Ohashi**, Shukutoku University, Japan; **Yongjun Park**, Sangji University, South Korea; **Donald Patnaude**, Ajarn Donald's English Language Services, Thailand; **Virginia Peng**, Ritsumeikan University, Japan; **Suangkanok Piboonthamnont**, Rajamangala University of Technology, Thailand; **Simon Pitcher**, Business English Teaching Services, Japan; **John C. Probert**, New Education Worldwide, Thailand; **Do Thi Hoa Quyen**, Ton Duc Thang University, Vietnam; **John P. Racine**, Dokkyo University, Japan; **Kevin Ramsden**, Kyoto University of Foreign Studies, Japan; **Luis Rappaport**, Cung Thieu Nha Ha Noi, Vietnam; **Lisa Reshad**, Konan Daigaku Hyogo, Japan; **Peter Riley**, Taisho University, Japan; **Thomas N. Robb**, Kyoto Sangyo University, Japan; **Rory Rosszell**, Meiji Daigaku, Japan; **Maria Feti Rosyani**, Universitas Kristen Indonesia, Indonesia; **Greg Rouault**, Konan University, Japan; **Chris Ruddenklau**, Kindai University, Japan; **Hans-Gustav Schwartz**, Thailand; **Mary-Jane Scott**, Soongsil University, South Korea; **Dara Sheahan**, Seoul National University, South Korea; **James Sherlock**, A.P.W. Angthong, Thailand; **Prof. Shieh**, Minghsin University of Science & Technology, Xinfeng; **Yuko Shimizu**, Ritsumeikan University, Japan; **Suzila Mohd Shukor**, Universiti Sains Malaysia, Malaysia; **Stephen E. Smith**, Mahidol University, Thailand; **Moon-young Son**, South Korea; **Seunghee Son**, Anyang University, South Korea; **Mi-young Song**, Kyungwon University, South Korea; **Lisa Sood**, VUS, BIS, Vietnam; **Jason Stewart**, Taejon International Language School, South Korea; **Brian A. Stokes**, Korea University, South Korea; **Mulder Su**, Shih-Chien University, Kaohsiung; **Yoomi Suh**, English Plus, South Korea; **Yun-Fang Sun**, Wenzao Ursuline College of Languages, Kaohsiung; **Richard Swingle**, Kansai Gaidai University, Japan; **Sanford Taborn**, Kinjo Gakuin Daigaku, Japan; **Mamoru Takahashi**, Akita Prefectural University, Japan; **Tran Hoang Tan**, School of International Training, Vietnam; **Takako Tanaka**, Doshisha University, Japan; **Jeffrey Taschner**, American University Alumni Language Center, Thailand; **Matthew Taylor**, Kinjo Gakuin Daigaku, Japan; **Michael Taylor**, International Pioneers School, Thailand; **Kampanart Thammaphati**, Wattana Wittaya Academy, Thailand; **Tran Duong The**, Sao Mai Language Center, Vietnam; **Tran Dinh Tho**, Duc Tri Secondary School, Vietnam; **Huynh Thi Anh Thu**, Nhatrang College of Culture Arts and Tourism, Vietnam; **Peter Timmins**, Peter's English School, Japan; **Fumie Togano**, Hosei Daini High School, Japan; **F. Sigmund Topor**, Keio University Language School, Japan; **Tu Trieu**, Rise VN, Vietnam; **Yen-Cheng Tseng**, Chang-Jung Christian University, Tainan; **Pei-Hsuan Tu**, National Cheng Kung University, Tainan City; **Hajime Uematsu**, Hirosaki University, Japan; **Rachel Um**, Mok-dong Oedae English School, South Korea; **David Underhill**, EEExpress, Japan; **Ben Underwood**, Kugenuma High School, Japan; **Siriluck Usaha**, Sripatum University, Thailand; **Tyas Budi Utami**, Indonesia; **Nguyen Thi Van**, Far East International School, Vietnam; **Stephan Van Eycken**, Kosei Gakuen Girls High School, Japan; **Zisa Velasquez**, Taihu International School/Semarang International School, China/Indonesia; **Jeffery Walter**, Sangji University, South Korea; **Bill White**, Kinki University, Japan; **Yohanes De Deo Widyastoko**, Xaverius Senior High School, Indonesia; **Dylan Williams**, SNU, South Korea; **Jisuk Woo**, Ichean University, South Korea; **Greg Chung-Hsien Wu**, Providence University, Taichung; **Xun Xiaoming**, BLCU, China; **Hui-Lien Yeh**, Chai Nan University of Pharmacy and Science, Tainan; **Sittiporn Yodnil**, Huachiew Chalermprakiet University, Thailand; **Shamshul Helmy Zambahari**, Universiti Teknologi Malaysia, Malaysia; **Ming-Yuli**, Chang Jung Christian University, Tainan; **Aimin Fadhlee bin Mahmud Zuhodi**, Kuala Terengganu Science School, Malaysia;

 Shirley F. Akis, American Culture Association/Fomara; **Gül Akkoç**, Boğaziçi University; **Seval Akmeşe**, Haliç University; **Ayşenur Akyol**, Ege University; **Ayşe Umut Aribaş**, Beykent University; **Gökhan Asan**, Kapadokya Vocational College; **Hakan Asan**, Kapadokya Vocational College; **Julia Asan**, Kapadokya Vocational College; **Azarvan Atac**, Piri Reis University; **Nur Babat**, Kapadokya Vocational College; **Feyza Balakbabalar**, Kadir Has University; **Gözde Balikçi**, Beykent University; **Deniz Balım**, Haliç University; **Asli Başdoğan**, Kadir Has University; **Ayla Bayram**, Kapadokya Vocational College; **Pinar Bilgiç**, Kadir Has University; **Kenan Bozkurt**, Kapadokya Vocational College; **Yonca Bozkurt**, Ege University; **Frank Carr**, Piri Reis; **Mengü Noyan Çengel**, Ege University; **Elif Doğan**, Ege University; **Natalia Donmez**, 29 Mayis Üniversite; **Nalan Emirsoy**, Kadir Has University; **Ayşe Engin**, Kadir Has University; **Ayhan Gedikbaş**, Ege University; **Gülşah Gençer**, Beykent University; **Seyit Ömer Gök**, Gediz University; **Tuğba Gök**, Gediz University; **İlkay Gökçe**, Ege University; **Zeynep Birinci Guler**, Maltepe University; **Neslihan Güler**, Kadir Has University; **Sircan Gümüş**,

Kadir Has University; **Nesrin Gündoğu**, T.C. Piri Reis University; **Tanju Gurpinar**, Piri Reis University; **Selin Gurturk**, Piri Reis University; **Neslihan Gurutku**, Piri Reis University; **Roger Hewitt**, Maltepe University; **Nilüfer İbrahimoğlu**, Beykent University; **Nevin Kaftelen**, Kadir Has University; **Sultan Kalin**, Kapadokya Vocational College; **Sema Kaplan Karabina**, Anadolu University; **Eray Kara**, Giresun University; **Beylü Karayazgan**, Ege University; **Darren Kelso**, Piri Reis University; **Trudy Kittle**, Kapadokya Vocational College; **Şaziye Konaç**, Kadir Has University; **Güneş Korkmaz**, Kapadokya Vocational College; **Robert Ledbury**, Izmir University of Economics; **Ashley Lucas**, Maltepe University; **Bülent Nedium Uça**, Dogus University; **Murat Nurlu**, Ege University; **Mollie Owens**, Kadir Has University; **Oya Özağaç**, Boğaziçi University; **Funda Özcan**, Ege University; **İlkay Özdemir**, Ege University; **Ülkü Öztürk**, Gediz University; **Cassondra Puls**, Anadolu University; **Yelda Sarikaya**, Cappadocia Vocational College; **Müge Şekercioğlu**, Ege University; **Melis Senol**, Canakkale Onsekiz Mart University, The School of Foreign Languages; **Patricia Sümer**, Kadir Has University; **Rex Surface**, Beykent University; **Mustafa Torun**, Kapadokya Vocational College; **Tansel Üstünloğlu**, Ege University; **Fatih Yücel**, Beykent University; **Şule Yüksel**, Ege University;

 Amina Saif Mohammed Al Hashamia, Nizwa College of Applied Sciences, Oman; **Jennifer Baran**, Kuwait University, Kuwait; **Phillip Chappells**, GEMS Modern Academy, U.A.E.; **Sharon Ruth Devaneson**, Ibri College of Technology, Oman; **Hanaa El-Deeb**, Canadian International College, Egypt; **Yvonne Eaton**, Community College of Qatar, Qatar; **Brian Gay**, Sultan Qaboos University, Oman; **Gail Al Hafidh**, Sharjah Women's College (HCT), U.A.E.; **Jonathan Hastings**, American Language Center, Jordan; **Laurie Susan Hilu**, English Language Centre, University of Bahrain, Bahrain; **Abraham Irannezhad**, Mehre Aval, Iran; **Kevin Kempe**, CNA-Q, Qatar; **Jill Newby James**, University of Nizwa; **Mary Kay Klein**, American University of Sharjah, U.A.E.; **Sian Khoury**, Fujairah Women's College (HCT), U.A.E.; **Hussein Dehghan Manshadi**, Farhang Pajooh & Jaam-e-Jam Language School, Iran; **Jessica March**, American University of Sharjah, U.A.E.; **Neil McBeath**, Sultan Qaboos University, Oman; **Sandy McDonagh**, Abu Dhabi Men's College (HCT), U.A.E.; **Rob Miles**, Sharjah Women's College (HCT), U.A.E.; **Michael Kevin Neumann**, Al Ain Men's College (HCT), U.A.E.;

 Aldana Aguirre, Argentina; **Claudia Almeida**, Coordenação de Idiomas, Brazil; **Cláudia Arias**, Brazil; **Maria de los Angeles Barba**, FES Acatlan UNAM, Mexico; **Lilia Barrios**, Universidad Autónoma de Tamaulipas, Mexico; **Adán Beristain**, UAEM, Mexico; **Ricardo Böck**, Manoel Ribas, Brazil; **Edson Braga**, CNA, Brazil; **Marli Buttelli**, Mater et Magistra, Brazil; **Alessandra Campos**, Inova Centro de Linguas, Brazil; **Priscila Catta Preta Ribeiro**, Brazil; **Gustavo Cestari**, Access International School, Brazil; **Walter D'Alessandro**, Virginia Language Center, Brazil; **Lilian De Gennaro**, Argentina; **Mônica De Stefani**, Quality Centro de Idiomas, Brazil; **Julio Alejandro Flores**, BUAP, Mexico; **Mirian Freire**, CNA Vila Guilherme, Brazil; **Francisco Garcia**, Colegio Lestonnac de San Angel, Mexico; **Miriam Giovanardi**, Brazil; **Darlene Gonzalez Miy**, ITESM CCV, Mexico; **Maria Laura Grimaldi**, Argentina; **Luz Dary Guzmán**, IMPAHU, Colombia; **Carmen Koppe**, Brazil; **Monica Krutzler**, Brazil; **Marcus Murilo Lacerda**, Seven Idiomas, Brazil; **Nancy Lake**, CEL-LEP, Brazil; **Cris Lazzerini**, Brazil; **Sandra Luna**, Argentina; **Ricardo Luvisan**, Brazil; **Jorge Murilo Menezes**, ACBEU, Brazil; **Monica Navarro**, Instituto Cultural A. C., Mexico; **Joacyr Oliveira**, Faculdades Metropolitanas Unidas and Summit School for Teachers, Brazil; **Ayrton Cesar Oliveira de Araujo**, E&A English Classes, Brazil; **Ana Laura Oriente**, Seven Idiomas, Brazil; **Adelia Peña Clavel**, CELE UNAM, Mexico; **Beatriz Pereira**, Summit School, Brazil; **Miguel Perez**, Instituto Cultural, Mexico; **Cristiane Perone**, Associação Cultura Inglesa, Brazil; **Pamela Claudia Pogré**, Colegio Integral Caballito / Universidad de Flores, Argentina; **Dalva Prates**, Brazil; **Marianne Rampaso**, Iowa Idiomas, Brazil; **Daniela Rutolo**, Instituto Superior Cultural Británico, Argentina; **Maione Sampaio**, Maione Carrijo Consultoria em Inglês Ltda, Brazil; **Elaine Santesso**, TS Escola de Idiomas, Brazil; **Camila Francisco Santos**, UNS Idiomas, Brazil; **Lucia Silva**, Cooplem Idiomas, Brazil; **Maria Adela Sorzio**, Instituto Superior Santa Cecilia, Argentina; **Elcio Souza**, Unibero, Brazil; **Willie Thomas**, Rainbow Idiomas, Brazil; **Sandra Villegas**, Instituto Humberto de Paolis, Argentina; **John Whelan**, La Universidad Nacional Autonoma de Mexico, Mexico

CONTENTS

UNIT QUESTION

What makes someone admirable?

A Discuss these questions with your classmates.

1. Why do we like to read stories about admirable people?

2. Who do you admire? Why do you admire this person?

3. Look at the photo. What makes these people admirable?

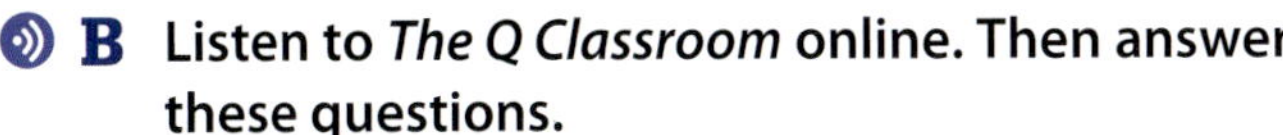

B Listen to *The Q Classroom* online. Then answer these questions.

1. Marcus says admirable people are brave and sacrifice themselves. What two examples does he give? Sophy says regular people can also be admirable. What examples does she give? What do you think makes someone admirable?

2. What qualities of an admirable person do Felix and Sophy discuss? Which qualities are most important in your opinion?

 **C** Go online to watch the video about the "big tipper." Then check your comprehension.

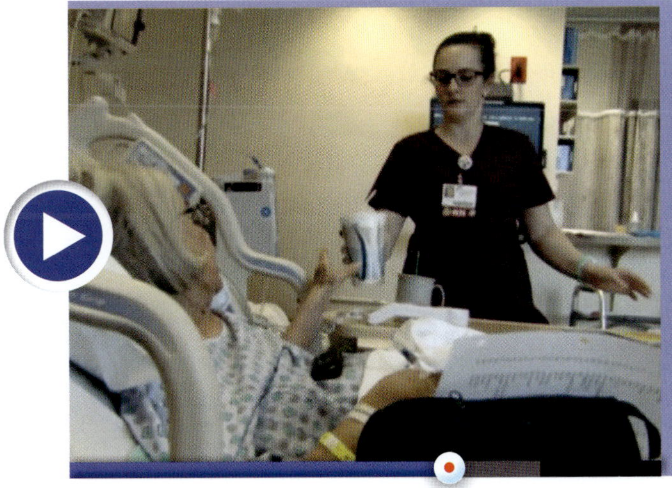

tuition *(n.)* the money that you pay to be taught, especially in a college or university

knight in shining armor *(n.)* a person who rescues another

tip *(n.)* a piece of information to help someone do something

tip *(n.)* money given to someone who performs a service for another

VIDEO VOCABULARY

 **D** Go to the Online Discussion Board to discuss the Unit Question with your classmates.

E Many different kinds of people have spoken about admirable qualities. Read the quotations below and discuss the following questions with a partner.

1. What does each quotation mean?

2. Do you agree with the quotation? Why or why not?

Words of Wisdom

1. Keep away from people who try to belittle your ambitions. Small people always do that, but the really great make you feel that you, too, can become great.

   —*Mark Twain, American author*

2. No person was ever honored for what he received. Honor has been the reward for what he gave.

   —*Calvin Coolidge, American President*

3. We must always remember with gratitude and admiration the first sailors who steered their vessels through storms and mists, and increased our knowledge of the lands of ice in the South.

   —*Roald Amundsen, Norwegian explorer*

4. I've learned that people will forget what you said, people will forget what you did, but people will never forget how you made them feel.

   —*Maya Angelou, American author*

F What qualities do you wish you had? In the chart, write down each quality and someone you know who has it. Share your ideas with your partner.

Quality	Name of person who has the quality

READING

READING 1 | We All Need a Role Model

You are going to read an essay about role models. Use the essay to gather information and ideas for your Unit Assignment.

PREVIEW THE READING

Reading Skill | Previewing and predicting

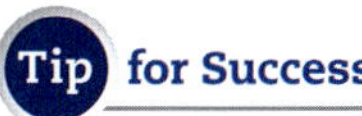

Tip for Success

When you write a research paper, you need to get information from a variety of sources. Previewing many books and articles will help you decide which ones are important for your research.

When you **preview** a text, you look through it quickly to learn general information. To preview:

- Read the title of the text.
- Look at any charts, graphs, pictures, or captions.
- Skim the text for subheadings. Subheadings indicate important ideas that will be developed in the text.

Previewing will help you **predict** what the text is about and prepare you to better understand it.

A. PREVIEW Read the title of the essay and look at the pictures. Write two things you think the text might be about.

1. ____

2. ____

B. Skim the essay and read the subheadings. Then look at the pairs of ideas below. Check (✓) one idea in each pair that you think might be developed in the text.

1. ☐ the qualities of role models
   ☐ a description of a specific role model

2. ☐ how people become role models
   ☐ what people may be role models

3. ☐ how role models can inspire us
   ☐ how we can inspire others

4. ☐ why role models do wrong things
   ☐ how role models learn from mistakes

C. Go online for more practice with previewing and predicting.

D. **QUICK WRITE** What qualities should a good role model possess? Write for 5–10 minutes in response. Be sure to use this section for your Unit Assignment.

E. **VOCABULARY** Check (✓) the words you know. Then work with a partner to locate each word in the reading. Use clues to help define the words you don't know. Check your definitions in the dictionary.

achievement (n.) 🔑	embody (v.)
acknowledged (for) (adj.) 🔑	inclined (adj.)
adversity (n.)	inherently (adv.)
aspire to (phr. v.)	pursue (v.) 🔑
confront (v.) 🔑	resolve (n.) 🔑
constrained (adj.)	version (n.) 🔑

🔑 Oxford 3000™ words

F. Go online to listen and practice your pronunciation.

WORK WITH THE READING

A. Read the essay and gather information about what makes someone admirable.

We All Need a Role Model

1   Who do you turn to when you have a problem or don't know how to do something? If you have someone to help you, you are lucky. If you have someone who takes a personal interest in helping you, you are luckier still. You have a role model.

Definition of a Role Model

2   Just what is a role model? First, let's recognize what it is not. It is not necessarily the smartest, strongest, or most successful person you know—although it could be. A role model is a person who has the characteristics you want for yourself and who can help you develop those traits. In other words, a role model both **embodies** positive qualities and teaches others, directly or through example.

Who Can Be a Role Model?

3   For most of us, our parents are our first role models. From when we are young children, they help us learn how to interact with other people—how to share, how to ask for what we need, and how to disagree without hurting someone. They are **inherently** interested in us and want us to do well. Furthermore, our parents teach us how to be adults in our society. A mother demonstrates to her daughters how to be a daughter, a woman, a wife, and a mother. Lessons learned from our parents will stay with us throughout our lives.

4   Other family members also serve as role models. Grandparents, uncles and aunts, cousins, and even siblings can show us how to manage our daily lives. Other obvious candidates include teachers and community leaders.

5   Sometimes we find role models in unexpected places. A family story might inspire us to have the same generosity as our grandfather had. We might see a young child fall, pick herself up, fall again, and pick herself up again. Her **resolve** might inspire us to continue in our own struggles, just as she learns to stand, keep her balance, and take a step. We might even find a model within ourselves, remembering back to a time when we were brave, or imagining a different **version** of ourselves who has the quality we desire.

What Role Models Do

6   Besides showing us how to do different things, a good role model also inspires us to **pursue** our dreams and **achievements**. A wise lawyer may inspire one person to study law, while a competent, compassionate physician may lead another person to the medical profession. Role models should empower others to become good parents, leaders, and members of society, and to internalize the qualities that they value. Therefore, role models must do the right thing, even when no one is watching, even when they won't be **acknowledged for** what they have done.

When Things Go Wrong

7   It is easy to be a role model when everything is going well, but it is perhaps more important to be a role model when things go wrong. A role model can show us how to handle **adversity**. For instance, we all make mistakes, but what do we do when we realize that we have made one? Do we try to hide it or pretend that it never happened? Are we **inclined** to look for someone to blame? Do we get angry?

8   A role model can show us how to deal with mistakes. A parent or teacher can help us repair any damage that was done or soothe any feelings that were hurt. He or she can listen to us, advise us on alternative courses of action, and support us as we make amends. The example of a community leader might serve to guide us toward appropriate action, encouraging us to imagine what he would do in our circumstances.

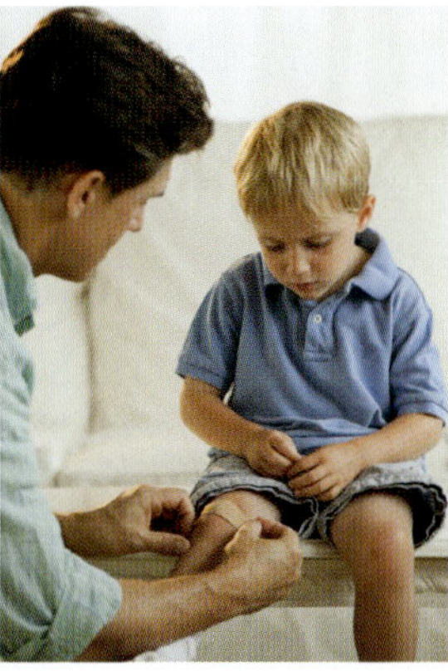

A role model shows us how to do different things and how to handle adversity.

9   Other situations that we might find ourselves in include dealing with stress, illness, or other misfortunes. **Confronting** these predicaments and overcoming them is made easier by the knowledge that people we admire and respect have faced similar conditions. Asking ourselves what they would do might help us be brave for a little while longer or figure out how to deal with life when we feel **constrained** by difficulties.

10   We need role models throughout our lives, and we only need to look around us to find someone who has experienced what we are going through, who has faced difficult decisions, or who has accomplished something we **aspire to** do. Sometimes we only have to look as far as the mirror to see a role model for our children, our neighbors, or even ourselves. Who is your role model? Maybe it is time to say thank you.

**Vocabulary
Skill Review**

Remember to read the
whole sentence and
consider the *context*.
This can help you
identify the correct
meaning of a word.

B. VOCABULARY **Here are some words and phrases from Reading 1.
Read the sentences. Then write each bold word or phrase next to the
correct definition. You may need to change verbs to their base form.**

1. My father **embodies** the quality of honesty; he never tells a lie.

2. The best athletes have the **resolve** to keep trying even when everything
   looks hopeless.

3. I will **pursue** my goal to be an engineer even though it will be difficult.

4. Winning the competition was an incredible **achievement** for such a
   young player.

5. When you set goals, don't be **constrained** by your present situation.
   If you can dream it, you can do it.

6. The athlete is suffering with a long-term injury, but he still **aspires
   to** race at the Olympics.

7. Skydiving is an **inherently** dangerous sport.

8. We all want to be **acknowledged for** our good deeds and the things we do
   to help others.

9. He had a hard life, but the **adversity** and challenges he faced made him a
   stronger person.

10. She had to **confront** the problem even though she was frightened.

11. I prefer my usual routine and am not **inclined** to try new things.

12. The first witness's **version** of the accident was quite different from the
    second witness's version.

a. ___________________ (*adj.*) recognized or shown appreciation for something

b. ___________________ (*n.*) a strong determination to do something

c. ___________________ (*adv.*) being a basic part of something that cannot
   be removed

d. ___________________ (*phr. v.*) to have a strong desire to do or become
   something

e. ___________________ (*adj.*) limited by something or someone

f. ___________________ (*n.*) a form of something that is different from
   another form of the same thing

g. ___________________ (*n.*) something that has been done successfully,
   especially through hard work or skill

h. _________________ (*v.*) to deal with a problem or difficult situation

i. ______*embody*______ (*v.*) to represent an idea or quality

j. _________________ (*adj.*) wanting to do something

k. _________________ (*n.*) a difficult or unpleasant situation

l. _________________ (*v.*) to try to achieve something over a period of time

iQ ONLINE **C.** Go online for more practice with the vocabulary.

D. Answer these questions.

1. What is the main idea of the essay? Write it in a complete sentence.

   ____

2. The main idea is found in two places. Where did you find the main idea?

   ____

E. Read the sentences. Number the main ideas in the order they are developed in the essay. (Use the subheadings in the essay to help you.)

____ a. Role models can show us how to deal with mistakes.

____ b. Role models can show us how to deal with problems.

__1__ c. A role model is a person with qualities that other people want to have.

____ d. Role models inspire us to develop our talents and abilities.

____ e. Many different kinds of people are role models.

F. Answer these questions.

1. Who are some of the people that can be role models?

   ____

2. How can a lawyer or doctor serve as a role model?

   ____

3. How can a role model help us deal with mistakes?

   ____

   ____

4. When is another time role models might help us?

____

____

G. Write _T_ (true) or _F_ (false) for each statement. Then correct each false statement to make it true. Write the paragraph number where you found information to support your answer.

____ 1. A role model is sometimes the most successful person you know.
(paragraph ____)

____

____ 2. A teacher is usually our first role model.
(paragraph ____)

____

____ 3. A young child can be a role model.
(paragraph ____)

____

____ 4. A role model is supposed to do the right thing.
(paragraph ____)

____

____ 5. A role model never makes mistakes.
(paragraph ____)

____

____ 6. We need role models only when we confront adversity.
(paragraph ____)

____

____ 7. It's hard to find a role model.
(paragraph ____)

____

____ 8. You can be your own role model.
(paragraph ____)

____

H. Complete the chart with two more people the essay identified as role models and what they can teach us.

Role models	What they can teach us
1. parents	1. how to interact with other people: -how to share -how to ask for what we need -how to disagree without hurting someone 2. how to be adults in our society
2.	
3.	

I. Go online to read *Taking Responsibility for Your Actions* and check your comprehension.

WRITE WHAT YOU THINK

A. Discuss these questions in a group.

1. Do athletes make good role models? Why or why not?

2. Who are you a role model for?

3. Imagine yourself 20 years from now. What would you like to hear people saying about you? What can you do between now and then so that people will say that?

B. Choose one question and write a paragraph in response. Look back at your Quick Write on page 6 as you think about what you learned.

READING 2 | Search for 100 Real-Life Heroes

You are going to read an article from the newspaper *The Guardian* about a journalist who spent two years searching for 100 real-life heroes. Use the article to gather information and ideas for your Unit Assignment.

PREVIEW THE READING

A. PREVIEW Read the title of the article and skim the first three paragraphs. Answer these questions.

1. What was Tithiya Sharma looking for?

____

2. Where was she looking?

____

3. How long did she look?

____

B. QUICK WRITE If you could do something to make your community better, what would you do? What would you need in order to accomplish this? Write for 5–10 minutes in response. Be sure to use this section for your Unit Assignment.

C. VOCABULARY Check (✓) the words you know. Use a dictionary to define any new or unknown words. Then discuss how the words will relate to the unit with a partner.

bear witness *(phr. v.)*	**inspirational** *(adj.)*
criteria *(n.)*	**navigate** *(v.)*
deconstruct *(v.)*	**notorious** *(adj.)*
disrupt *(v.)*	**pressing** *(adj.)*
drastic *(adj.)*	**reconciliation** *(n.)*
initiative *(n.)*	**underprivileged** *(adj.)*

 Oxford 3000™ words

 **D. Go online to listen and practice your pronunciation.**

WORK WITH THE READING

Search for 100 Real-Life Heroes

Indian Journalist Tithiya Sharma Visits 45 Countries over Two Years to Find Local Champions

by Kate Hodal and Tom Phillips

City of God favela in Rio de Janeiro, Brazil

1 Heroes are normally the stuff of mythology. But for Tithiya Sharma, whose journey to find them took two years and spanned 45 countries across six continents, heroes are part of everyday life.

2 Sharma spent the two years looking for 100 **inspirational** figureheads[1], community leaders, and social workers.

3 The only requirement? That these heroes were changing the future of their countries, from the clean boulevards of the west to the most **underprivileged** and conflict-ridden corners of the developing world.

4 Calling her quest the 100 Heroes Project, the New Delhi-born former journalist left the newsrooms of Mumbai, formerly Bombay, in May 2010 and in December 2011 touched down in South America, on one of the final stops on her global tour.

5 "I'd become so used to being a journalist in India, making really good money, renting a fancy apartment in the most expensive part of Bombay," says Sharma, 29, on her way to meet her latest hero in Rio de Janeiro's **notorious** City of God favela[2].

6 "It was such an easy trap to fall into and I knew that if I was going to make a change it had to be something really **drastic**. So I quit my job, sold all my stuff, moved back in with my parents, and decided I wanted to do this."

7 "This" means **navigating** her way alone through some of the world's trickiest corners, often with little more than a scrap of paper and some scribbled notes as her guide.

8 Sharma has no set **criteria** for her heroes, whom she finds by using Internet search engines and then relying on local contacts to determine the area's most **pressing** issues.

9 "What makes a hero, anyway? Is it that you're helping 1,000 people or two people?" she asks. "If you help the life of one single person but in a really meaningful way, I think you're a hero."

---

[1] **figureheads:** people in a high position in a country or organization but who have no real power or authority

[2] **favela:** a poor area in or near a Brazilian city, with many houses that are close together and in bad condition

10   Sharma's latest find—number "70-something," she says—is 50-year-old social worker Maria do Socorro Melo Brandão, a favela-born but university-educated psychiatrist who now runs City of God's Seed of Life Association.

11   The community group works with local job-seekers and offers extracurricular[3] activities to children and teens.

12   As Brandão describes her work providing counseling to slum[4] residents, Sharma underlines the effect just one individual can have on the rest of the world. "All it takes is that one person who takes it upon him or herself to put all of the pieces of the puzzle together, to inspire, to bring people together, that one person who doesn't give up," she says.

13   "Sometimes it's just about **deconstructing** the way people think. One amazing idea can **disrupt** the thinking of an entire community or country."

14   Determined to use "social media for social good," Sharma is raising money and awareness for the heroes she finds, using her journalistic background to blog, tweet, and publish articles about her experiences.

15   Donors have been impressed: while she has paid for her trip primarily through personal savings, Indian travel site MakeMyTrip has funded all her flights—its chief marketing officer, Mohit Gupta, says he was inspired by Sharma's drive to learn about and take in "the best the world has to offer."

16   Sharma admits that traveling alone has proven difficult at times. She has been in some dangerous situations, but these experiences have only strengthened her resolve.

17   Sharma notes that wherever she travels, she does so through the eyes of a woman, and in most situations, she feels wronged, unhappy, or unsettled by what she sees. "I now know I want to work in a women's rights organization," she says. She wants to work with and for the female heroes "in society who are clawing[5] every day to create a new normal."

18   By the end of her two-year journey, Sharma had seen the Northern Lights, churches of Lalibela, Ethiopia, and the pyramids of Egypt, crossed 45 countries over six continents, and found well over 100 heroes.

19   But only one thing stood out, she says. "After time, every church starts looking the same." What she remembers most about this trip is the people. Sharma talks about the love and hospitality she experienced everywhere she visited.

20   "It's a reminder of how lucky I am, how fortunate and privileged to be here and now and having this experience. To be able to **bear witness**. I could do this for the rest of my life."

Six of the 100 Heroes

Sonja Kruse (right) with a woman she met while writing her book, *The Ubuntu Girl*

---

[3] **extracurricular:** not part of the usual course of work or studies at a school or college

[4] **slum:** an area of a city that is very poor and where the houses are dirty and in bad condition

[5] **clawing:** slowly achieving something by using a lot of determination and effort

21 **Sonja Kruse** The 32-year-old "Ubuntu Girl" spent a year traveling through her native South Africa with nothing but a backpack, a camera, and 100 rand ($12.14) to prove that *ubuntu*—an African concept meaning "I am only because you are"—is alive and well. She is writing a book about her experiences.

22 **Yamam Nabeel** Iraqi-born, London-based Nabeel started FC Unity to bring together people from different social, religious, and ethnic backgrounds through soccer, and teach them to work as a team. Since its founding in 2006, the charity has created soccer-based education and development programs in Iraq, Sudan, England, and Ghana.

23 **Mahfuza Folad** From an office above a Kabul cookie shop, Folad serves as executive director of Justice for All Organisation, which offers free advice and support to Afghan women and works for women's and children's rights. Folad is also a judge in Kabul.

24 **Dr. Jo and Lyn Lusi** The husband and wife co-founded HEAL Africa, which provides medical and social care for women in Congo. Their charity heads one of Congo's three full-service hospitals and provides community-based **initiatives** such as safe houses and remote clinics, microlending schemes, and law-training programs.

25 **Felicite Rwemalika** The founder of the Association of Kigali Women in Sports, Rwemalika started Rwanda's first women's sports federation in 2001 to give young Hutu and Tutsi[6] girls a chance to find **reconciliation** in post-conflict Rwanda. Her organization also promotes women's rights and teaches healthy lifestyles and economic empowerment.

---

[6] **Hutu and Tutsi:** two ethnic groups inhabiting Rwanda and Burundi in Africa

B. **VOCABULARY** Work with a partner. Read the bold word or phrase and the three definitions in each row. Two of the definitions are similar and correct. A third is incorrect. Cross out the incorrect definition.

	a.	b.	c.
1. **inspirational** *(adj.)*	a. making someone want to be better or more successful	b. causing someone to have exciting new ideas	c. ~~making someone breathe~~
2. **underprivileged** *(adj.)*	a. having the position of power just below the manager	b. having less money and fewer opportunities than most people	c. not having rights or advantages that most people have
3. **pressing** *(adj.)*	a. needing to be dealt with immediately	b. required to complete a task	c. urgent

4. **notorious** *(adj.)*	**a.** well known for being bad	**b.** knowing a lot of bad words	**c.** famous for doing something wrong
5. **drastic** *(adj.)*	**a.** extreme in a sudden, serious way	**b.** hard to do	**c.** very different from normal
6. **navigate** *(v.)*	**a.** to sail on a ship	**b.** to find the direction you need to go in	**c.** to use a map to decide how to travel
7. **criteria** *(n.)*	**a.** principles used to help make a decision	**b.** rules for accepting or not accepting something	**c.** knowledge
8. **deconstruct** *(v.)*	**a.** to tear something down	**b.** to analyze something to understand it	**c.** to figure out how something works
9. **disrupt** *(v.)*	**a.** to make it difficult for something to continue in the normal way	**b.** to cause something to stop or change course	**c.** to hurt something without meaning to
10. **bear witness** *(phr. v.)*	**a.** to provide evidence of the truth of something	**b.** to experience something and tell others about it	**c.** to solve problems that other people can't
11. **initiative** *(n.)*	**a.** a plan for achieving a goal	**b.** a ceremony that makes a person a member of a group or organization	**c.** a plan for dealing with a problem
12. **reconciliation** *(n.)*	**a.** restarting a friendship that ended because of distance	**b.** an end to a disagreement and beginning of an agreement	**c.** the start of a good relationship after a fight

C. Go online for more practice with the vocabulary.

D. Answer these questions.

1. How did Tithiya Sharma decide if someone was a hero?

    ____

2. What are two ways Sharma's decision to go on her journey changed her life?

    ____

3. Why did Sharma choose Maria do Socorro Melo Brandão as a hero?

    ____

4. Of the six heroes featured at the end of the article, which has the greatest
    influence on their community? Why?

    ____

    ____

5. What does Tithiya Sharma plan to do after her journey?

    ____

**E. Write _T_ (true) or _F_ (false) for each statement. Then correct each false
statement to make it true. Write the paragraph number where you found
information to support your answer.**

____ 1. Tithiya Sharma paid for her journey by herself.
         (paragraph ___)

____

____ 2. Sharma sometimes found herself in dangerous areas with just a few
         notes to guide her.
         (paragraph ___)

____

____ 3. Sharma provided counseling to slum residents in the City of God favela.
         (paragraph ___)

____

____ 4. Sharma tried to raise money for the 100 heroes by writing about them.
         (paragraph ___)

____

___ **5.** Mahfuza Folad runs a cookie shop in Kabul.
(paragraph ___)

____

___ **6.** Sharma's best memories of her journey are of the places she visited
around the world.
(paragraph ___)

____

F. **Complete the chart with information about the heroes from the article.**

Name	Country	Why he/she is a hero
Maria do Socorro Melo Brandão		
	South Africa	
	England/Iraq	Created soccer-based education and development programs in Iraq, Sudan, England, and Ghana to teach people of different social, religious, and ethnic backgrounds to work as a team.
Mahfuza Folad		
Dr. Jo and Lyn Lusi		
	Rwanda	

G. **Based on the chart above, what will be the lasting effects of each hero's actions for his or her community? Compare your ideas with a partner.**

1. Maria do Socorro Melo Brandão

____

____

2. Sonja Kruse

____

____

3. Yamam Nabeel

____

____

4. Mahfuza Folad

____

____

5. Dr. Jo and Lyn Lusi

____

____

6. Felicite Rwemalika

____

____

WRITE WHAT YOU THINK

A. Discuss the questions in a group. Look back at your Quick Write on page 12 as you think about what you learned.

1. Have you ever volunteered to do something to help your community? If so, describe your experience.

2. Firefighters are often seen as admirable. What other people are seen as admirable because of their profession? Why?

3. How can you become a local champion? How could your actions help your community?

B. Think about the unit video, Reading 1, and Reading 2 as you discuss the questions. Then choose one question and write a paragraph in response.

1. Think of someone in the news who is a real-life role model. What makes this person a role model?

2. If you did something for your community, would you want to be publicly acknowledged for it? Why or why not?

Vocabulary Skill　Using the dictionary

When you look up a word in the dictionary, you will find the definition and other information about the word and how it is used. Different dictionaries may include slightly different information, but they are generally organized in a similar way. Notice the different parts of this dictionary entry from the *Oxford Advanced American Dictionary for learners of English.*

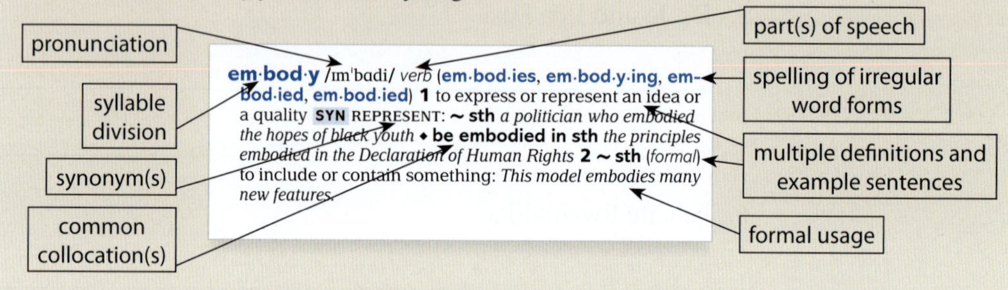

All dictionary entries are from the *Oxford Advanced American Dictionary for learners of English* © Oxford University 2011.

A. Look at the dictionary entry for *mentality*. Check (✓) the information that this entry has.

> men·tal·i·ty **AWL** /mɛnˈtæləti/ noun [usually sing.] (pl. men·tal·i·ties) the particular attitude or way of thinking of a person or group SYN MINDSET: *I cannot understand the mentality of video gamers.* ♦ *a criminal/ghetto mentality* ➔ see also SIEGE MENTALITY

☐ syllable division

☐ pronunciation

☐ part(s) of speech

☐ spelling of irregular word forms

☐ multiple definitions

☐ example sentences

☐ formal usage

☐ synonym(s)

☐ common collocation(s)

B. Look at the dictionary entries. Answer the questions. Then compare your answers with a partner.

con·front /kənˈfrʌnt/ *verb*
1 ~ **sb/sth** (of problems or a difficult situation) to appear and need to be dealt with by someone: *the economic problems confronting the country* ◆ *The government found itself confronted by massive opposition.* **2** ~ **sth** to deal with a problem or difficult situation **SYN** FACE UP TO: *She knew that she had to confront her fears.* **3** ~ **sb** to face someone so that they cannot avoid seeing and hearing you, especially in an unfriendly or dangerous situation: *This was the first time he had confronted an armed robber.* **4** ~ **sb with sb/sth** to make someone face or deal with an unpleasant or difficult person or situation. **5** **be confronted with sth** to have something in front of you that you have to deal with or react to: *When confronted with a bear, stop and stay calm.*

1. How many definitions does *confront* have? _____

2. What synonym is given for *confront*? ____________________

3. What common expression is given that uses *confront*?

   ____

in·her·ent AWL /ɪnˈhɪrənt; -ˈhɛr-/ *adj.* ~ **(in sb/sth)** that is a basic or permanent part of someone or something and that cannot be removed **SYN** INTRINSIC: *the difficulties inherent in a study of this type* ◆ *Violence is inherent in our society.* ◆ *an inherent weakness in the design of the machine* ▶ **in·her·ent·ly** AWL *adv.*: *an inherently unworkable system*

4. What part of speech is *inherent*? ____________________

   Inherently? ____________________

5. What synonym is given for *inherent*? ____________________

6. Where are the syllable divisions in *inherently*? Write the word and put

   a slash (/) after each syllable. ____________________

con·strain AWL /kən'streɪn/ *verb* (*formal*) **1** [usually passive] **~ sb to do sth** to force someone to do something or behave in a particular way: *The evidence was so compelling that he felt constrained to accept it.* **2** [often passive] to restrict or limit someone or something: **~ sth** *Research has been constrained by a lack of funds.* ◆ **~ sb (from doing sth)** *She felt constrained from continuing by the threat of losing her job.*

7. In what form is *constrain* usually used? ________________

8. How many example sentences are given for *constrain*? ____

9. What words often follow *constrain*? ________________

a·chieve·ment 🔑 AWL /ə'tʃiːvmənt/ *noun* **1** [C] a thing that someone has done successfully, especially using their own effort and skill: *the greatest scientific achievement of the decade* ◆ *It was a remarkable achievement for such a young player.* ◆ *They were proud of their children's achievements.* ⊃ collocations at ACHIEVE **2** [U] the act or process of achieving something: *the need to raise standards of achievement in education* ◆ *Even a small success gives you a sense of achievement* (= a feeling of pride).

10. Where are the syllable divisions in *achievement*? Write the word and

    put a slash (/) after each syllable. ________________

11. How many definitions does *achievement* have? ____

12. What common collocation is given that uses *achievement*?

    ____

C. Work with a partner. Look up words from Reading 1 and Reading 2 in your dictionary. Take turns asking questions like the ones in Activity B.

iQ ONLINE **D.** Go online for more practice with using the dictionary.

WRITING

UNIT OBJECTIVE At the end of this unit, you will write an analysis essay about the qualities that make someone admirable. This essay will include specific information from the readings, the unit video, and your own ideas.

Writing Skill | Organizing and developing an essay

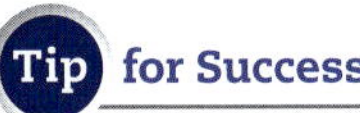 **for Success**

The writer is responsible for producing text that others can understand. Write on one topic (unity) in a logical way (coherence).

An **analysis essay** examines a topic by breaking it down into smaller parts. Remember that an essay includes an **introduction**, one or more **body paragraphs**, and a **conclusion**.

Introduction

This paragraph should make the reader interested in your topic. It usually includes a "hook" to catch the reader's attention. It also provides background information or general statements about the topic. Within the introduction paragraph, include a **thesis statement**. The thesis statement contains the topic and the **controlling idea** (a specific idea or an opinion about the topic) of the essay. It tells the reader the purpose of the essay.

        topic   controlling idea

Thesis statement: A role model inspires people to do their best.

Body paragraphs

For each body paragraph, include a **topic sentence** that states the topic of the paragraph and the controlling idea. Add supporting sentences that provide as much detail as possible to fully develop your thesis. Use supporting sentences that all relate to or develop the topic to create **unity**. Organize the supporting sentences in a logical way so there is a clear connection between the ideas to create **coherence**. Often **transition words** like *first*, *in addition*, and *for example* are used to show the relationship between supporting ideas.

Conclusion

The conclusion brings the essay to a close. This paragraph may restate the thesis statement in different words, summarize the main points, or do both. Write sentences that remind the reader of why he or she is reading the essay. You can also use the conclusion to help your reader look beyond the essay or think about further ideas that relate to your topic.

Successful People

Are fame and fortune in your future? Do you dream of becoming a billionaire or a famous actor? For most of us, that is not too likely. Even though we may never see our picture on the cover of a glossy magazine, we all want to make something of ourselves and have a good life. We all want to succeed, and identifying what qualities make someone successful can help us to achieve that goal.

Successful people share three common qualities that allow them to stand out. First, people who are successful are organized. They don't waste time, and they work in ways that maximize their efficiency. They also work longer hours. Second, they are focused and single-minded. They can see where they want to go and only do the things that will get them there. For example, when they are working on something, they don't get lost in the details or overwhelmed by the tasks they need to do. Finally, people who are successful must be able to set and accomplish goals. Knowing what they want helps them stay both organized and focused.

If you want to be successful, you need to get organized, stay focused, and set and accomplish goals. Not many people succeed without these qualities, but don't despair. These behaviors can be learned and improved, and anyone can stand out if he or she develops organization, focus, and goals.

1. Read the introduction again. Circle the hook.

2. Find the thesis statement in the introductory paragraph. Underline the topic once. Underline the controlling idea twice.

3. Underline the topic sentence of the body paragraph.

4. One sentence in the body doesn't contribute to the unity of the essay because it doesn't develop the topic. Draw a line through it.

5. Circle the transition words that contribute to the coherence of the body paragraph.

6. Read the conclusion again. Circle the answer that best describes what the conclusion does.
   a. It restates the thesis statement and suggests further examination of the topic.
   b. It summarizes the main points and suggests ways to be successful.
   c. It restates the thesis statement and summarizes the main points.

B. **In the chart on page 25, list two people you consider successful, the qualities you believe contributed to their success, and their accomplishments. List one family member or friend and a famous or well-known person.**

Successful people	Qualities	Accomplishments
my mother	hardworking, organized, caring	worked as a nurse while raising my sisters and me

C. Work with a partner. Read the sentences and number them to make a meaningful body paragraph. First, identify the topic sentence. Then order the supporting sentences to create unity and coherence. Then write the whole paragraph in order and check for unity and coherence.

____ a. First, role models have a well-developed set of skills or qualities, but they may be unwilling or unable to help others develop them.

____ b. Mentors, on the other hand, may have the same skills or qualities, but they make it a point to train or teach others on a personal basis.

____ c. There are two important differences between role models and mentors.

_3_ d. For example, a research scientist may be great in the lab but not in the classroom.

____ e. Role models may or may not pay personal attention to those they inspire and may affect a large number of people at once, but mentors always have a few special people they work with individually.

____ f. A role model can inspire many people just by his or her actions, while a mentor is limited to inspiring a few people at a time.

____ g. This is because of the time it takes to work with someone individually.

____ h. A second factor is the number of people a role model or mentor can influence at one time.

D. The paragraph in Activity C is the body paragraph for an essay about role models and mentors. Answer the questions.

1. List some possible hooks for an introduction to this paragraph.

____

____

2. Choose the best thesis statement for the essay.
    a. We all need both role models and mentors.
    b. Role models and mentors are both admirable, but their effect on our lives will be very different.
    c. Both role models and mentors are admirable.

3. What is the best way to conclude this essay?

____

 **E.** Go online for more practice with organizing and developing an essay.

1. Restrictive relative clauses* describe or identify nouns. Usually, they directly follow nouns, noun phrases, or indefinite pronouns (*something*, *everyone*, etc.).

pronoun /
noun   adjective clause

A role model is <u>someone</u> **who makes a difference in people's lives.**
Role models face <u>questions</u> **that we may also face.**

2. Most relative clauses begin with a relative pronoun.

- Use *who* or *that* after nouns for people.

Role models are <u>people</u> **who may volunteer in their communities.**
<u>Ordinary people</u> **that we each know** can be role models.

- Use *that* or *which* after nouns for things. (*Which* usually sounds more formal.)

<u>Biographies</u> **that tell stories of successful people** are very popular.
Role models do <u>things</u> **that we would like to do.**
Sarah works for a <u>company</u> **which helps the homeless.**

3. You can think of a sentence with a relative clause as a combination of two sentences about the same noun.

- In a **subject relative clause**, the relative pronoun stands for the subject of the clause. It is followed by a verb.

A role model is someone. + ~~He or she~~ makes a difference in people's lives. =

subject + verb

A role model is <u>someone</u> **who makes a difference in people's lives.**

- In an **object relative clause**, the relative pronoun stands for the object of the clause. The relative pronoun is followed by a subject + verb.

Role models face questions. + We may also face ~~the questions~~. =

object + subject + verb

Role models face <u>questions</u> **that we may also face.**

4. In object relative clauses, the relative pronoun can be omitted.

<u>Ordinary people</u> ~~that~~ **we each know can be role models.**
Role models do <u>things</u> ~~that~~ we **would like to do.**

*Also called *identifying adjective clauses*

A. Underline the relative clause in each sentence. Circle the noun, noun phrase, or indefinite pronoun it identifies.

1. Not every person who makes his or her community a better place is acknowledged for it.

2. They do the things that they do because they want to make their communities better.

3. At 19, Ahmed borrowed a novel that changed his life forever.

4. His father was an illiterate cattle merchant who insisted that his son have an education.

5. She reads storybooks to children who have no access to television.

6. Lisa started a youth environmental group which is trying to clean up the city.

7. The trash Lisa's group collects is carried away by bicycles.

B. Combine each pair of sentences using a restrictive relative clause with *who*, *that*, or *which*. Use the words in bold to help you.

1. We all aspire to do **something**. Other people will respect **it**.

   We all aspire to do something that other people will respect.

2. Role models may inspire us to help **people**. **They** cannot help themselves.

   ____

3. Role models have **qualities**. We would like to have **them**.

   ____

4. To me, **a person** is a role model. **He** inspires others to do good deeds.

   ____

5. Reading novels gives students **something**. They cannot get **it** in textbooks.

   ____

6. Caring for the environment is **something**. We can all do **it**.

   ____

7. **Someone** is a generous person. **He or she** donates money to charity.

   ____

C. Which sentences in Activity B can omit the relative pronoun?
Cross out the relative pronoun if it can be omitted.

D. Go online for more practice with restrictive relative clauses.

E. Go online for the grammar expansion.

Unit Assignment · Write a three-paragraph analysis essay

In this assignment, you are going to write a three-paragraph analysis essay. As you prepare your essay, think about the Unit Question, "What makes someone admirable?" Use information from Reading 1, Reading 2, the unit video, and your work in this unit to support your essay. Refer to the Self-Assessment checklist on page 30.

Go to the Online Writing Tutor for a writing model and alternate Unit Assignments.

PLAN AND WRITE

A. BRAINSTORM Follow these steps to help you organize your ideas.

1. In the chart below, list three people who you think are admirable. Describe the qualities that they possess and give an example of their accomplishments.

Person	Qualities	Accomplishments
1.		
2.		
3.		

2. Compare the people in your chart. What qualities do they share? How are their accomplishments similar or different?

Similarities	Differences

Outlines help you put your ideas in order. Often when you write an outline for an essay, you include the thesis statement, notes about supporting ideas for your body paragraphs, and notes for the concluding paragraph.

B. **PLAN** **Follow these steps to plan your essay.**

1. Write a topic for your essay.

   ____

2. Write an opinion or a specific idea about the topic above. This will be your controlling idea for your thesis statement.

   ____

   ____

3. Now combine your topic from 1 and your controlling idea from 2 to form your thesis statement.

   ____

   ____

   ____

4. Go to the Online Resources to download and complete the outline for your analysis essay.

C. **WRITE** Use your **PLAN** notes to write your essay. Go to *iQ Online* to use the Online Writing Tutor.

1. Write your analysis essay about the qualities that make a person admirable. Be sure to have an introduction, a body paragraph, and a conclusion. Include restrictive relative clauses where appropriate. You may also use transition words from the box below to help connect your ideas.

In addition,	For example,	First,	Finally,
Also,	For instance,	Second,	Most importantly,

2. Look at the Self-Assessment checklist below to guide your writing.

REVISE AND EDIT

A. **PEER REVIEW** Read your partner's essay. Then go online and use the Peer Review worksheet. Discuss the review with your partner.

B. **REWRITE** Based on your partner's review, revise, and rewrite your essay.

C. **EDIT** Complete the Self-Assessment checklist as you prepare to write the final draft of your essay. Be prepared to hand in your work or discuss it in class.

	SELF-ASSESSMENT	
Yes	**No**	
☐	☐	Does the essay have an introduction with a hook and thesis statement?
☐	☐	Are there enough details in the body paragraph to support the topic sentence?
☐	☐	If transition words are included, are they used appropriately?
☐	☐	Are relative clauses used correctly?
☐	☐	Does the essay include vocabulary from the unit?
☐	☐	Did you check the essay for punctuation, spelling, and grammar?

D. **REFLECT** Go to the Online Discussion Board to discuss these questions.

1. What is something new you learned in this unit?

2. Look back at the Unit Question—What makes someone admirable? Is your answer different now than when you started the unit? If yes, how is it different? Why?

TRACK YOUR SUCCESS

Circle the words and phrases you have learned in this unit.

Nouns
achievement 🔑 AWL
adversity
criteria 🔑 AWL
initiative 🔑 AWL
reconciliation
resolve 🔑 AWL
version 🔑 AWL

Verbs
confront 🔑
deconstruct
disrupt
embody
navigate
pursue 🔑 AWL

Phrasal Verbs
aspire to
bear witness

Adjectives
acknowledged (for) 🔑 AWL
constrained AWL
drastic
inclined AWL
inspirational
notorious
pressing
underprivileged

Adverb
inherently AWL

🔑 Oxford 3000™ words
AWL Academic Word List

Check (✓) the skills you learned. If you need more work on a skill, refer to the page(s) in parentheses.

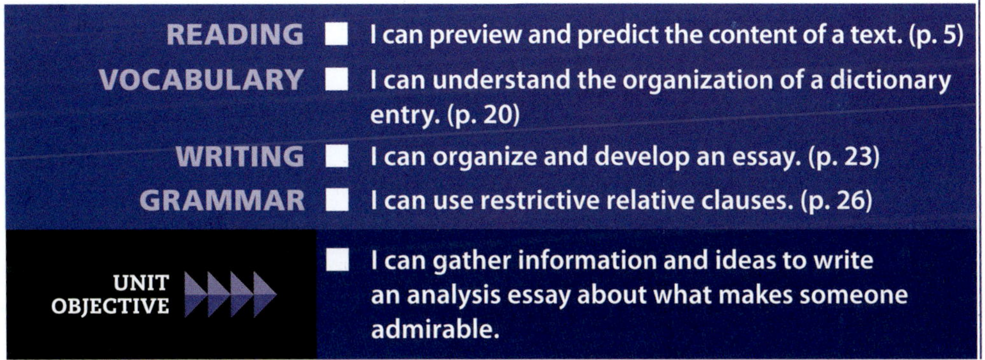

UNIT QUESTION

What makes you want to buy something?

A Discuss these questions with your classmates.

1. What sorts of things do you like to shop for? What do you not enjoy shopping for?

2. How does the way something appears influence your decision to buy it?

3. Look at the photo. Would you buy something from this shop? Why or why not?

B Listen to *The Q Classroom* online. Then answer these questions.

1. Why are appearances important to Sophy when she makes a purchase? Do you share this value? Why or why not?

2. What does Marcus say about packaging and Felix about presentation? Give other examples of how packaging or presentation affects your decision to buy something.

 **C** Go to the Online Discussion Board to discuss the Unit Question with your classmates.

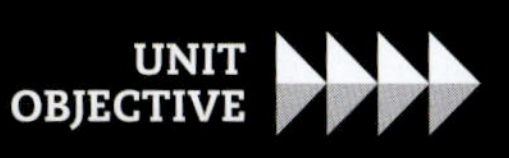

UNIT OBJECTIVE Read an article from a business journal and an article from a design magazine and gather information and ideas to write a descriptive essay about a product, business, or service.

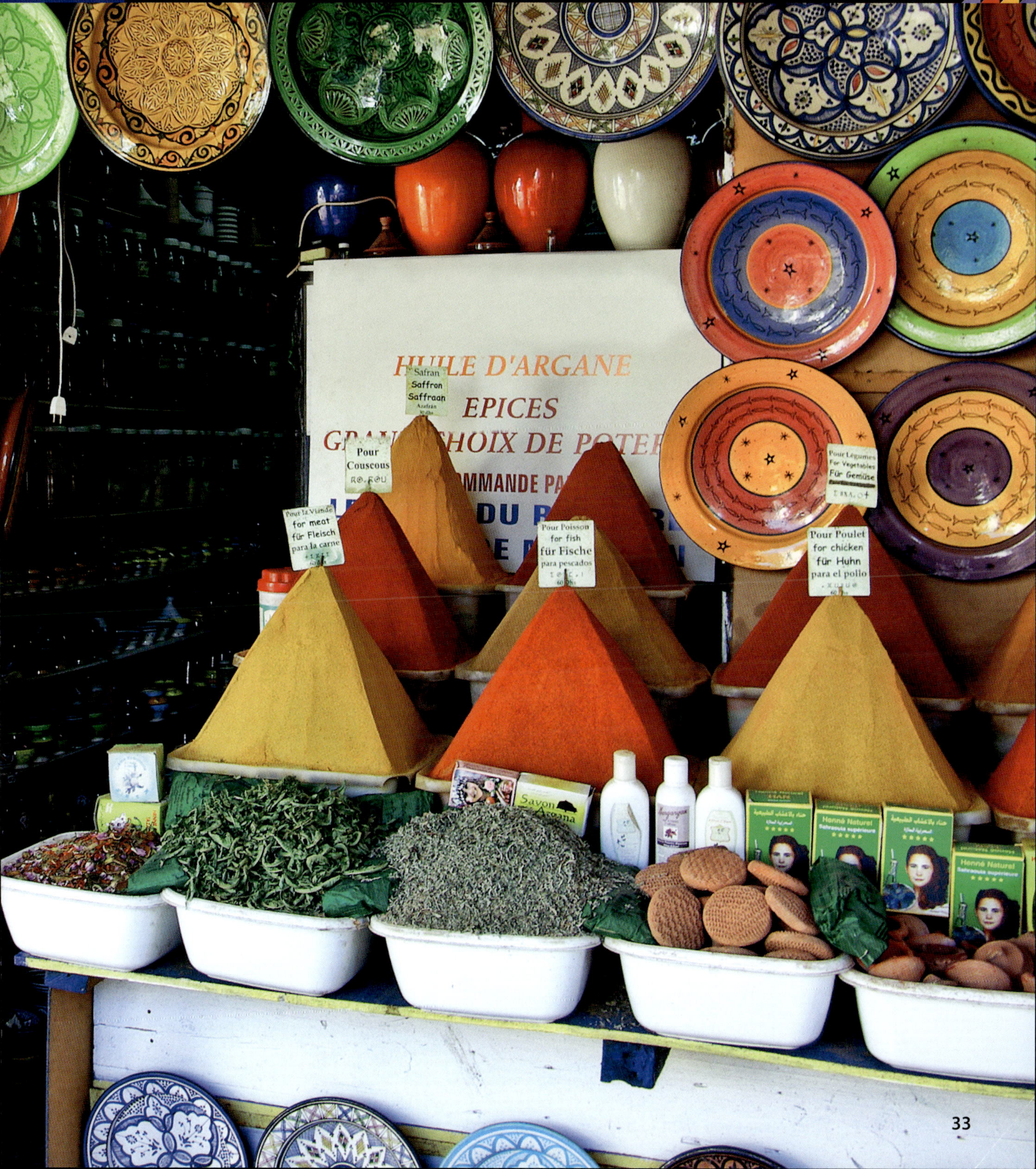

D Complete the questionnaire about your recent shopping purchases.
Write down or check (✓) your answers. Then compare with a partner.

What was the last thing you bought because . . . ?	Item or service bought	Don't remember	Doesn't apply
1. you needed to satisfy a basic need (like food or medicine)		☐	☐
2. you had to replace something that was broken		☐	☐
3. you needed it for school		☐	☐
4. you were in a hurry (even though it wasn't exactly what you wanted)		☐	☐
5. the price was lower than it was before		☐	☐
6. you were bored and wanted something to do		☐	☐
7. you thought it was stylish or special		☐	☐
8. all your friends had one		☐	☐

E Read the descriptions of different kinds of shoppers below and discuss
these questions with your partner.

1. Which descriptions sound like you and your partner?

2. Are you one specific type of shopper or a combination of types?

The practical shopper: You always go shopping with a list and only buy the
things you need.

The convenient shopper: You only go shopping if something is easy to get or
especially affordable.

The emotional shopper: You shop more often when you are happy or sad.

The trendy shopper: You typically buy stylish things or popular brand names.

The peer-pressure shopper: You often buy things because your friends are
buying them.

READING 1 | So Much Dead Space

You are going to read an article from a business journal about how store windows are used to attract customers. Use the article to gather information and ideas for your Unit Assignment.

PREVIEW THE READING

Paco Underhill

A. PREVIEW Read the title and subtitle of the article by Paco Underhill, the CEO of a research firm that focuses on the relationships between people and stores and people and products. Answer these questions.

1. What does the title mean?

2. What do you think Paco Underhill thinks about most store windows?

3. Based on the subtitle, what is Underhill's purpose in writing the article?

B. QUICK WRITE Think about stores you typically pass by or shop in. What kinds of things do you usually see in the windows? Describe what is in a favorite store window. Write for 5–10 minutes in response. Be sure to use this section for your Unit Assignment.

C. VOCABULARY Check (✓) the words you know. Then work with a partner to locate each word in the reading. Use clues to help define the words you don't know. Check your definitions in the dictionary.

allude to *(phr. v.)*	**liberate** *(v.)*
concept *(n.)* 🔑	**pedestrian** *(n.)*
distinguish *(v.)* 🔑	**priority** *(n.)* 🔑
evolve *(v.)*	**promote** *(v.)* 🔑
focus on *(phr. v.)* 🔑	**sophisticated** *(adj.)*
individual *(n.)* 🔑	**urban** *(adj.)* 🔑

🔑 Oxford 3000™ words

D. Go online to listen and practice your pronunciation.

WORK WITH THE READING

So Much Dead Space
Creating Store Windows Alive with Promise

1   I am a nerdy American researcher. No one has ever thought of me as fashionable. What I do know about is shops and shopping. I've always been good at watching people. Because I grew up with a terrible stutter[1] and was not comfortable talking, I learned to *observe* as a way of understanding social rules. I've turned this coping mechanism[2] into a profession. What I have done for the past twenty-five years is research shopping behavior: I simply walk around malls and shopping streets and figure out what motivates people to buy things. What makes someone stop and look at a store window? What makes someone go into a store? What makes someone buy something?

2   As I stroll around, I look closely at store windows, since they are an essential part of the shopping experience. In his delightful book *Made in America*, Bill Bryson writes about the history of stores and shopping in America. He describes the big store windows that were an important feature of most retail stores in the past century. When I look out my office window in New York City, I see many of those windows. They remain the same today as they were some 120 years ago.

a store window display

3   A century ago, people took the time to stop and look into store windows. I imagine them walking along slowly, stopping at a tall window, and peering through the glass to see the latest fashions and newest products. Today, strolling, window-shopping **pedestrians** are an old-fashioned **concept**. Most people look straight ahead and walk with a quick, determined gait[3]. Everyone seems to be in a hurry. They walk a lot faster now than they did in the old days.

4   Throughout modern times, different factors have changed the way pedestrians walk in busy **urban** areas. One of the most significant of these factors is traffic lights. William H. Whyte, the American author and urbanist[4], wrote about the pattern and movement of pedestrians on the sidewalk. He observed that because traffic lights are timed for the speed of cars, people pile up on street corners as they wait for the light to change. When the light changes, that "pile" of people will cross and stay crowded together as they continue down the street. Behind them, there will be a "gap" of fewer people, but then another crowd will form when the traffic light changes again. This creates a pattern of crowds and gaps on urban shopping streets.

---

[1] **stutter:** difficulty speaking because you cannot stop yourself from repeating the first sound of some words

[2] **coping mechanism:** a technique to deal with a difficult matter or situation

[3] **gait:** a way of walking

[4] **urbanist:** a person who studies cities

5   Now, think about how **individuals** behave when walking in these crowds of people. Some people will speed up to get out of the crowd, and then the entire group will begin to walk more quickly. This behavior affects how people view the store windows that they pass by. Even if you wanted to slow down or stop to look in a window, you couldn't. You have to keep walking quickly so that you won't be in the way of other people. That's why window displays need to instantly grab attention. But many don't. Take the drugstores in my neighborhood, for example. The windows are filled with boxes of bleach and detergent, packages of razors and soap, and whatever else can be squeezed into the space. With the window so crowded, it is impossible to **focus on** any single product. Often, it's difficult to even see clearly what is really being **promoted**! Maybe in 1928, it was important for a store to advertise the large selection of products offered. Maybe then, shoppers had the time to really take a look at a window and examine the display. But these days, retailers are lucky if pedestrians just glance at their store windows.

6   The way our eyes and brain handle information has become more **sophisticated**. Thanks to television and computers, our ability to process images is faster. We no longer read letter by letter but rather in groups of words at a time. TV programs have **evolved** so that we see the stories of years— or even lifetimes—in just a few hours. A billboard can tell a more sophisticated joke today than it could 20 years ago. A 15-second commercial can **allude to** a full story. Likewise, when it comes to window displays, shoppers today can understand information more quickly.

7   Store windows today must be quick reads. They must be simple enough so that the products can be clearly identified, and they must be creative enough to catch the busy pedestrian's eye. Just a quick look at a store window should answer many questions for savvy[5] shoppers: Who is the core market[6] of the store? Does the store fit their personal style or not? How long will a typical trip into the store take? Especially since today's retail market is so competitive, if done right, windows can function as an important brand-identity[7] tool. As retailers, you must know who your customers are, and you must create windows that they will understand. For instance, Kiehl's, which sells all-natural bath and body products, uses its windows as a place for highlighting social issues, which fits with the **priorities** of its customers.

> *Especially since today's retail market is so competitive, if done right, windows can function as an important brand-identity tool.*

8   My favorite windows are in France. A man who runs his family's boutique off the main square in Strasbourg takes enormous pleasure in his windows. They tell jokes. Some are related to history. Sometimes his windows make me chuckle. The clothes are part of a larger story. His store always **distinguishes** itself from the other shops on the crowded square because his windows always make an impression. As busy as I might be as I walk down the street, his windows make me stop. Even more, they almost always tempt me to come inside the shop and take a good look around.

9   So what can stores do with their "dead space"? How can windows come alive? To modern retailers, I propose the following: Let's **liberate** our design teams. Stop filling windows with products. Tell a story. Make us laugh. Make us think. Learn from advertisers like Calvin Klein or Benetton who think outside the box with ads that catch our attention and motivate a response. Windows can be like literature. It's OK if not everybody understands the story you're telling. What is important is that the target customer gets it, and stops to look.

---

[5] **savvy:** having practical knowledge of something
[6] **core market:** the main group of people a store sells to

[7] **brand identity:** characteristics that quickly identify and distinguish a brand to shoppers

B. **VOCABULARY** Here are some words and phrases from Reading 1. Read the sentences. Circle the answer that best matches the meaning of each bold word or phrase.

1. On a typical weekday, the sidewalks are filled with **pedestrians** who are window-shopping or looking for a place to stop and eat.
   a. people walking
   b. people bicycling

2. His **concept** for the advertisement was poorly thought out, so the design team chose another.
   a. product
   b. idea

3. Unlike quiet streets in rural areas, the crowded streets in **urban** areas are often filled with people.
   a. city
   b. country

4. Each **individual** in the survey was a professional designer.
   a. group of people
   b. single person

5. In a crowded store, it is easy to get overwhelmed and not be able to **focus on** what you like.
   a. concentrate
   b. remember

6. Because the business **promoted** its products successfully on the Internet, they sold well.
   a. developed
   b. advertised

7. After a year of study abroad, I had a more **sophisticated** view of the world.
   a. able to understand complicated ideas
   b. knowledgeable about a specific topic

8. Her poetry has **evolved** over the years because she has gained more confidence and developed her own style.
   a. kept the same form
   b. changed from an earlier form

9. She **alluded to** her work experience when she said, "I've been very busy the past few years."
   a. spoke indirectly about
   b. avoided speaking about

10. I had a lot to do and not much time, so I decided what my **priorities** were and I did those things first.
    a. the most important things
    b. the easiest things

11. The store **distinguishes** itself from its competitors by having lower prices.
    a. copies
    b. differs

12. Knowledge can **liberate** people and give them independence.
    a. control
    b. set free

C. Go online for more practice with the vocabulary.

D. Answer these questions.

1. What is the topic of the reading?

   ____

2. What is the controlling idea?

   ____

   ____

E. Circle the answer that best completes each statement.

1. The author is a researcher who ____.
   a. creates window displays
   b. observes how people shop
   c. compares shopping at different stores

2. The main reason that the article describes urban pedestrians is to ____.
   a. explain why store windows must be both simple and creative
   b. analyze their walking patterns
   c. contrast modern shoppers with shoppers in the past

3. The author thinks store windows should show ____.
   a. the products we can buy inside
   b. a piece of history
   c. something that catches our attention

4. The idea of "dead space" refers to ____.
   a. how the brain handles information from TV programs and billboards
   b. store windows that don't attract attention
   c. the empty space between pedestrians on the sidewalk

5. The author's intended audience is ____.
   a. shoppers
   b. pedestrians
   c. store owners

F. **Answer these questions.**

1. How is pedestrian behavior different now than in the last century?

   ____

2. What happens on sidewalks when people have to stop and wait for traffic lights to change?

   ____

3. What is the problem with the drugstore windows in the author's neighborhood?

   ____

4. What is one example the author uses to show how "our ability to process images is faster"?

   ____

5. What does the author mean when he says that store windows must be "quick reads"?

   ____

6. What does the author like about his favorite store windows? Give two examples.

   ____

G. **The article refers to the work and research of others. Find the names of two authors and three stores in the reading. Complete the chart.**

Name	Information about the author or store	Reason to include in the reading
Bill Bryson		
	author and urbanist	
	store selling all-natural bath and body products	
Calvin Klein		
Benetton		

H. Answer these questions.

1. According to Paco Underhill, what are seven things store windows should be and do?

   1. ____

   2. ____

   3. ____

   4. ____

   5. ____

   6. ____

   7. ____

2. What is one thing a store window should not be or do?

   ____

I. Go online to read *Think Before You Buy* and check your comprehension.

WRITE WHAT YOU THINK

A. Discuss these questions in a group.

1. Other than store windows, what are some ways store owners use appearance inside the store to attract customers?

2. Given that online shopping is more and more common, stores create online "windows" on their websites. How is shopping different when browsing or "window-shopping" online?

3. Think about a favorite store or website. Describe what is in the store window or on the website. Based on what you read, is the store window or website appealing? Explain.

B. Choose one question and write a paragraph in response. Look back at your Quick Write on page 35 as you think about what you learned.

Critical Thinking Tip

The Write What You Think questions require you to discuss your ideas. Through **discussion**, you can clarify your understanding of new material, which will help you remember it better. Discussion also helps you clarify information for others who may not understand it.

The purpose of **highlighting** and **annotating** is to identify important ideas in a text. Both of these techniques will allow you to quickly find the information later, without having to reread the text.

Highlighting

Always decide the purpose of your highlighting before you begin. Then highlight, underline, or circle information in a text such as:

- the main idea or topic of a paragraph
- key words, details, or examples
- phrases that summarize the information

Use different-colored highlighter pens for different types of information. For example, use one color for main ideas and another for details. Or use a graphic system, such as solid lines, dotted lines, circling, etc.

Annotating

Annotating—writing directly on the page of a text—is a useful way to identify and mark important information. First, read a paragraph and decide what is important. Then write brief notes in the margin. You may use abbreviations such as:

T = thesis	S = summary	R = reason
MI = main idea	Ex = example	? = question

A. Read this paragraph from Reading 1 and look at the highlighting and annotations. Then answer the questions below.

S = people understand info faster now

    The way our eyes and brain handle information has become more sophisticated. Thanks to television and computers, our ability to process images is faster. We no longer read letter by letter but rather in groups of words at a time. TV programs have evolved so that we see the stories of years—or even lifetimes—in just a few hours. A billboard can tell a more sophisticated joke today than it could 20 years ago. A 15-second commercial can allude to a full story. Likewise, when it comes to window displays, shoppers today can understand information more quickly.

R = TV, computers

1. What does the information highlighted in yellow show?

2. What does the information highlighted in pink show?

3. What purposes do the two annotations have?

B. Highlight and annotate a paragraph from Reading 1 on page 43. Follow these steps. Then compare your notes with a partner.

1. Highlight in one color (or circle) the main idea of the paragraph.

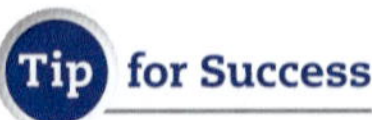

Tip for Success

After annotating the text, you may want to write out your notes to use as a reference and study tool.

2. Highlight in another color (or underline) the key details.

3. Write a brief note in the margin to summarize the paragraph.

4. Write a note in the margin that identifies a specific example.

Store windows today must be quick reads. They must be simple enough so that the products can be clearly identified, and they must be creative enough to catch the busy pedestrian's eye. Just a quick look at a store window should answer many questions for savvy shoppers: Who is the core market of the store? Does the store fit their personal style or not? How long will a typical trip into the store take? Especially since today's retail market is so competitive, if done right, windows can function as an important brand-identity tool. As retailers, you must know who your customers are, and you must create windows that they will understand. For instance, Kiehl's, which sells all-natural bath and body products, uses its windows as a place for highlighting social issues, which fits with the priorities of its customers.

C. Go online for more practice highlighting and annotating.

READING 2 | Now on Stage: Your Home!

You are going to read an article from a design magazine about how to "stage" a home: how to make it more attractive to people who might buy it. Use the article to gather information and ideas for your Unit Assignment.

PREVIEW THE READING

A. **PREVIEW** Read the title of the article and look at the photos. Which room do you think is staged? Why?

before

after

B. **QUICK WRITE** Which version of the room do you like more? Write for 5–10 minutes in response. Include a description to help your reader form a mental picture. Be sure to use this section for your Unit Assignment.

C. **VOCABULARY** Check (✓) the words you know. Use a dictionary to define any new or unknown words. Then discuss how the words will relate to the unit with a partner.

feature (v.) 🔑	minimize (v.)	remove (v.) 🔑
in theory (idm.) 🔑	negative (n.) 🔑	residence (n.)
investment (n.) 🔑	neutral (adj.)	tend (v.) 🔑
mentally (adv.) 🔑	potential (adj.) 🔑	visualize (v.)

🔑 Oxford 3000™ words

D. Go online to listen and practice your pronunciation.

WORK WITH THE READING

A. Read the article and gather information about what makes you want to buy something.

Now on Stage: Your Home!

by Douglas Nan

1   Tina Miller is busy at work in the kitchen of her New Jersey condominium[1], wrapping dishes in paper. Just outside, several large boxes stand near the front door, and in the living room, Miller's two sons are packing video games. "We've been here for almost ten years," she says, looking around. "I never realized how much stuff we had."

2   Two months ago, Tina's husband Evan accepted a job in another state, and now the family is getting ready to move. "There's a lot of work to do, but the hardest part seems to be selling this condo," she explains. "We've had it on the market[2]

for over a month and several people have come to see it. But so far, no luck."

3   **In theory**, the Millers' home should have sold quickly. It is in a modern building on a quiet street; shops and restaurants are within walking distance. The couple has even reduced the sale price by $10,000. Connie Tran, the real estate agent[3] working with the Millers, believes she knows what the problem is. "This is a nice condo. The rooms are large and there's lots of light, but the feel of the place is all wrong. The living room is full of boxes; the kitchen and bathroom are cluttered[4]; the paint on the walls is too dark. It doesn't make a great first impression on **potential** buyers."

4   To help sell their condo, Tran has suggested that the Millers hire someone to stage it. What exactly

---

[1] **condominium** (short form: **condo**): an apartment that is owned by the person who lives in it
[2] **on the market**: for sale
[3] **real estate agent**: a person who sells homes
[4] **cluttered**: messy and disorganized; filled with many things

does this mean? The main goal, professional stagers would say, is to prepare a house to sell by making it as attractive as possible. For most people, this simply involves fixing things that are broken or cleaning a place thoroughly. But even though these things are important, real estate agent Elizabeth Weintraub says that staging goes "beyond decorating and cleaning. It's about creating [a] mood[5]. Staging makes your house look bigger, brighter, cleaner, warmer, and best of all, it makes home buyers want to buy it."

5 The Millers have agreed to have their home staged. So what will a professional home stager suggest doing to help sell their condo?

6 1. *Minimize the clutter.* The Miller family has lived in their home for ten years, and though they are preparing to move, many of the rooms are still full of furniture, books, electronics, and other things that people collect over time. These things can make the place look crowded and smaller than it is. Packing and moving most of the unnecessary items out of the condo will make it look much larger—which will appeal to buyers.

7 2. *Store personal items.* The Millers also have to be aware of the small stuff: photos and magazines in the living room, a child's drawings on the refrigerator, and slippers in the bathroom. Not only do these things make the condo appear more cluttered, they also make it look like the *Millers'* home— and that's a problem. A buyer doesn't want to tour the place and see someone else's stuff. Professional home stager Barb Schwartz advises sellers to "clear all unnecessary objects throughout the house." Doing this will help a potential buyer to "**mentally** 'move in' with their own things"—and to **visualize** themselves in the home.

8 3. *Organize what's left.* Once each room is down to a few essential items, a professional stager will make sure these things are positioned in an attractive way that makes the rooms look good. Sandra Rinomato, the host of a popular TV show about selling houses, offers these suggestions:

- "**Feature** only a few pieces of furniture [in each room] and pull pieces away from walls to make rooms look bigger."

- "Bedrooms are difficult to stage because they are in daily use." To make these rooms appear spacious[6] and neat, Rinomato recommends using white sheets on the bed and "clearing everything off nightstands."

- "Open the drapes[7] or **remove** them completely. Light, bright rooms give the impression of a happy place—and everyone wants to move into a happy place."

9 4. *Repaint if necessary.* Four years ago, the Millers painted the walls in the living room a warm reddish color. They love it but a potential home buyer might not, for a couple of reasons. The color was a personal choice made by the Millers— which makes the condo still seem as if it is theirs. Dark colors can also make a room appear smaller. Repainting the walls a lighter, more **neutral** color will make the room look more spacious.

10 What if the Millers don't sell the condo before they move? Should they still have it staged if it is empty? Sveta Melchuk, of Home

---

[5] **mood:** a feeling

[6] **spacious:** open, with lots of room

[7] **drapes:** thick curtains used to cover windows

Staging Montreal, and many other real estate professionals say yes. Melchuk notes on her website that "most people have a hard time imagining [a] space as a potential home if it contains no furniture. The rooms will look too big or too small" and may invite buyers to "notice the **negatives**" (such as a scratch on the floor or old windows). For these reasons, many real estate agents will recommend furnishing some of the main rooms in a vacant home.

11   In some cases, staging a home can cost as much as $4,000, which has many sellers wondering if it's worth it. Barb Schwartz, who has staged thousands of **residences**, believes it is. According to her, the average home can take up to 212 days to sell, while a professionally staged one usually takes just 37. Schwartz and others in her field[8] also note that homes they prepare for viewing **tend** to sell for more money—often thousands of dollars more.

12   Ultimately, staging seems to be a good **investment**, especially if an owner is having difficulty selling a home. The Millers agree. "I hardly recognize this place anymore," laughs Tina. "It looks wonderful—like something you'd see in a magazine. And last week, we had two offers to buy. The trouble is, I like it here so much now that I don't want to move!"

[8] **field:** a profession or area of work (for example, the medical field)

B. **VOCABULARY** Complete the sentences with the vocabulary from Reading 2.

feature (v.)	mentally (adv.)	neutral (adj.)	residence (n.)
in theory (idm.)	minimize (v.)	potential (adj.)	tend (v.)
investment (n.)	negative (n.)	remove (v.)	visualize (v.)

1. Close your eyes and try to _________________ this room full of furniture. Can you picture it?

2. The yellow paint on these walls is too bright. A(n) _________________ color like tan or cream would be better.

3. Can you _________________ the books and papers from the table and put them in your backpack?

4. We really like the apartment. The only _________________ is that it doesn't come with parking.

5. They own a home in the country, but their primary _________________ is in London.

6. Most people in this city _________________ to live in apartments. Only a few live in large houses.

7. One way to ________________ noise in the apartment is to put rugs on the floors. Then it will be quieter.

8. I can think of two ________________ ways to use this room: as an office or as an extra bedroom.

9. This month's *House* magazine is going to ________________ photos of famous people's homes.

10. Shopping for a new home can be ________________ exhausting. Sometimes you get so tired, you can't think anymore.

11. Buying a house is a good ________________. You can live in it now and sell it later.

12. ________________, it should only take twenty minutes to rearrange my furniture, but I always take hours to think about where everything should go.

 C. Go online for more practice with the vocabulary.

D. Circle the correct answer. Then explain more about your answer.

1. Who is the intended audience for this article?
   a. people selling a home
   b. new homeowners
   c. potential home buyers

   Why did you choose this answer?

   ____

2. People hire a professional home stager primarily to help them ___ a home.
   a. find and buy
   b. organize and decorate
   c. find a buyer for

   According to Elizabeth Weintraub, what is the most important thing a home stager can do?

   ____

3. Look at the numbered list in paragraphs 6–9. A good subheading for this section of the article would be ___.
   a. Four Reasons You Should Hire a Professional Home Stager
   b. Four Tips for Successfully Staging a Home
   c. Four Staging Mistakes Many Homeowners Make

   Why are there bullet points in paragraph 8?

   ____

4. Paragraph 10 describes why ___.
   a. it's helpful to stage a vacant home
   b. staged houses sometimes do not sell
   c. empty homes are easier to sell

   Where in paragraph 10 is this idea explicitly stated?

   ____

5. The purpose of paragraph 11 is to explain ___ a home.
   a. the cost of staging
   b. the time it takes to stage
   c. the benefits of staging

   Why does Barb Schwartz believe that paying for staging is worthwhile?

   ____

6. The author ends the article by saying he ___ home staging is a good idea.
   a. believes
   b. doesn't think
   c. isn't sure if

   The author uses an example to support this idea. What is surprising about
   the example?

   ____

E. Answer these questions about the Miller family.

1. Who are the Millers?

   ____

2. Why are they selling their home?

   ____

3. What are some good points about their home?

   ____

4. What are some things that are wrong with the Millers' home?

   ____

   ____

5. What did the Millers do to increase the chances of selling their home?

   ____

6. Were their efforts effective? How do you know?

____

7. Why do you think the author included the Millers in this article?

____

F. The article describes different home staging techniques. Complete the chart with the correct information.

Home staging technique	Reason for doing it
1. Pack and move unnecessary items out of the home.	*makes a place look larger*
2. Remove personal items from the rooms.	
3.	makes rooms look bigger
4. Use white sheets in the bedroom.	
5.	makes rooms seem bright and happy
6. Paint walls a neutral color.	
7. Furnish some of the main rooms in an empty home.	

WRITE WHAT YOU THINK

A. Discuss the questions in a group. Look back at your Quick Write on page 44 as you think about what you learned.

1. Draw a picture of one of the rooms in your home in as much detail as possible. Then look again at the tips in Reading 2. What changes would you need to make so that the room was more attractive to a potential buyer?

2. Do you think a stager's job is interesting? Could you do it? Why or why not?

B. Before you watch the video, discuss the question in a group.

1. In your opinion, what were the most important suggestions in the reading for staging a home?

2. What are some other suggestions for staging a home?

C. **Go online to watch the video about staging homes. Then check your comprehension.**

accentuate *(v.)* to emphasize something to make it noticeable

commodity *(n.)* a product that can be bought or sold

enlist *(v.)* to persuade someone to help

languish *(v.)* to suffer something unpleasant for a long time

D. **Think about the unit video, Reading 1, and Reading 2 as you discuss the questions. Then choose one question and write a paragraph in response.**

1. Reading 1 ends with "It's OK if not everybody understands the story you're telling. What is important is that the target customer gets it, and stops to look." What story do home sellers want to tell?

2. What lesson from staging a home could window designers use? How would that idea need to be modified to fit a store window instead of a home?

Vocabulary Skill   Collocations with nouns

Collocations are words that often occur together. While there are no rules to help you learn collocations, it is important to pay attention to the patterns of words in a text. These patterns are clues that show you which words collocate. There are several common collocation patterns with nouns.

Adjective + noun

Does the store fit the shopper's **personal style** or not?

Most people have a **hard time** imagining a space as a potential home if it contains no furniture.

Verb + noun/noun phrase

Maybe in the past, shoppers had the time to really **take a look** at a window.

The condo doesn't **make a great first impression** on potential buyers.

Preposition + noun/noun phrase

Everyone seems to be **in a hurry**.

In theory, the Millers' home should have sold quickly.

A. Circle the word that usually goes together with the noun in each sentence. Look back at Reading 1 (R1) and Reading 2 (R2) to check your answers.

a shopping mall

1. (**Social / Society**) **rules** tell people what behavior is acceptable. (R1, para. 1)

2. In **the** (**old / past**) **days**, no one researched how people shop. (R1, para. 3)

3. There have been many changes to advertising in (**current / modern**) **times**. (R1, para. 4)

4. A good advertisement should (**grab / grasp**) **the shopper's attention**. (R1, para. 5)

5. The mover can only carry two boxes (**at / by**) **a time**. (R1, para. 6)

6. We had a feeling that we weren't hearing the (**full / total**) **story**. (R1, para. 6)

7. A book in the window (**caught / held**) **his eye**, so he went into the store. (R1, para. 7)

8. The house was not attractive, so the buyers only took a (**sudden / quick**) **look** at it. (R1, para. 7)

9. While some people (**have / take**) **pleasure** in shopping, many others hate it. (R1, para. 8)

10. The latest computer technology has just come (**at / on**) **the market**. (R2, para. 2)

11. Stores try to (**create / make**) **a mood** using displays and lighting. (R2, para. 4)

12. (**During / Over**) **time**, the value of most homes will increase. (R2, para. 6)

13. You can only take two (**personal / private**) **items** on a plane. (R2, para. 7)

14. The salesperson gave advice (**in / on**) **a way** that was helpful and practical. (R2, para. 8)

15. Light-colored walls (**make / give**) **the impression** of a large living space. (R2, para. 8)

16. She is one of the best researchers (**in / of**) **her field**. (R2, para. 11)

Tip **for Success**

Some collocations are **idioms**. This means that when the words are combined, they take on a unique meaning. Some examples of idioms are *window-shopping* and *in theory*.

B. Choose five collocations from Activity A. Write a sentence for each.

I like to have the newest computer technology on the market.

C. Go online for more practice with collocations with nouns.

WRITING

UNIT OBJECTIVE ▶▶▶▶ At the end of this unit, you will write a descriptive essay about a product, business, or service. This essay will include specific information from the readings, the unit video, and your own ideas.

Writing Skill | Writing a descriptive essay

A **descriptive essay** describes a person, place, or thing in a way that gives the reader a clear mental picture of the subject of the essay.

Organization

- The **introduction** should make the reader interested in what you are describing. It should include a **thesis statement** that tells why the person, place, or thing is your focus.
- Write one or more **body paragraphs** that contain the details of your description.
- Finish with a **conclusion** that gives your final thoughts or opinion about what you are describing.

Descriptive language

A good descriptive essay gives a clear mental picture of the subject of the essay. The reader should be able to imagine that he or she is with the person described, at the place described, etc. Include strong **imagery** (language that helps create these mental pictures) in your body paragraphs.

Not descriptive

She walked into the room.

He was dressed formally.

The street was filled with people selling food.

Descriptive

She walked **slowly** and **nervously** into the **dark** room.
  (with adjectives and adverbs)

He wore **a light suit, a tie, and shiny shoes.**
  (with details and specific language)

The street was filled with **loud men shouting out orders above the smoky smell of grilling meat.**
  (with sensory language related to sounds, smells, etc.)

My Favorite Restaurant

One of my favorite restaurants is Ben's Diner on Fourth Street because it's perfect for a casual, delicious meal. Ben's is a family business that has been serving the local community for over sixty years. Look for their red neon sign with its flashing knife and fork. When you see it, you know you can expect good food that was cooked with fresh, local ingredients.

As soon as you step through the door at Ben's, you'll be glad you came. The restaurant is brightly lit and spotlessly clean, with gleaming tables and sparkling floors. You'll get a warm welcome from one of the staff, who will take you to a comfortable seat. I like the soft red leather seats in the booths, or sometimes I sit at the smooth marble counter. The pleasant noise of conversation and the soothing clatter of dishes will surround you. If you're not already hungry, the rich smell of homemade chicken soup coming from the kitchen will get you ready to eat.

Ben's menu has some old favorites and some unexpected surprises. Their perfectly grilled burger is made of 100% prime beef. Served on a soft toasted bun, it's crunchy on the outside and moist and peppery inside. Add some sharp cheddar cheese for a satisfying treat. Their Greek salad is famous for its fresh ingredients: bright green lettuce leaves, deep red tomatoes, and tangy purple olives. Or how about chicken fajitas, served beside your table in a sizzling skillet, with a spicy aroma I can't resist?

So, whether you're looking for somewhere new to get some great food or just passing through, I suggest you head over to Ben's. You'll feel right at home and enjoy some good cooking, too.

1. Underline the thesis statement and the concluding sentence.

2. Find at least two sensory details for each sense.

    a. sight: _red neon sign,_ _______________________

    b. sound: _______________________

    c. taste: _______________________

    d. smell: _______________________

    e. touch: _______________________

B. Read the sentences. Rewrite them to make them more descriptive. Add adjectives and adverbs, details and specific language, and sensory language. Be creative.

1. The man lived in a house far from the city.

   The old man lived quietly in a small farmhouse far from the busy city.

2. The room was filled with roses, daisies, and lilacs.

   ____

3. The chicken and potatoes were good.

   ____

4. We went on a hike though the forest.

   ____

5. His aunt entered the room.

   ____

6. I didn't get to watch the soccer game on TV.

   ____

C. **WRITING MODEL** Read the model descriptive essay. Then answer the questions on page 55.

Adventure Seekers Wanted

Do you live for your next escape from your everyday routine? Are you a strong and healthy outdoor person seeking your next great adventure? The Adventurer sport utility vehicle (SUV) is the right vehicle to buy for adventure and outdoor fun if you are a thrill-seeking, athletic person who spends time outdoors. The Adventurer is the best, most reliable SUV to take you, your thrill-seeking friends, and all your gear where you're going, and it will get you there in great comfort and style.

Do you spend time climbing snow-capped mountains, rafting through red rock canyons on a raging river, or cruising the rocky shoreline of a vast ocean seeking the perfect wave? If you answered yes to any of these questions, then you know that you need to be driving a powerful, all-wheel-drive vehicle to arrive at your destination. The new Adventurer delivers that power and maneuverability. Don't be fooled by the quiet, comfortable ride. The new Adventurer is the perfect off-road vehicle. It is a powerful, all-wheel-drive vehicle that is as at home on steep,

---

rough dirt roads as it is on a flat, smooth highway. And, as a hybrid, it is the environmentally friendly vehicle you want to drive.

Do you plan to take friends and need to carry a lot of gear to your next adventure? There is plenty of room for all the equipment you'll need. The interior of the Adventurer is roomy and comfortable, so you can bring along as many as five fun-loving friends. The seats, of the softest, finest-quality leather, will keep you cool in the heat of the summer and warm in the winter. The climate control air system keeps the interior at a steady, regulated temperature.

Each adventure seeker creates his or her own story. Whatever your story, the Adventurer is the means to get you there. You will want the Adventurer because it is the right choice for your healthy, active lifestyle. Test-drive yours today!

1. What is the product?

   ____

2. What is the controlling idea about the product?

   ____

3. Who is the target customer for the product?

   ____

4. What makes the product appealing?

   ____

   ____

   ____

5. What does the conclusion do?

   ____

6. Can you form a mental picture of the Adventurer SUV? Explain your answer.

   ____

   ____

   ____

D. Below is a cluster diagram the author used to organize the description of the Adventurer. Complete the cluster diagram with ideas from the essay and your own ideas.

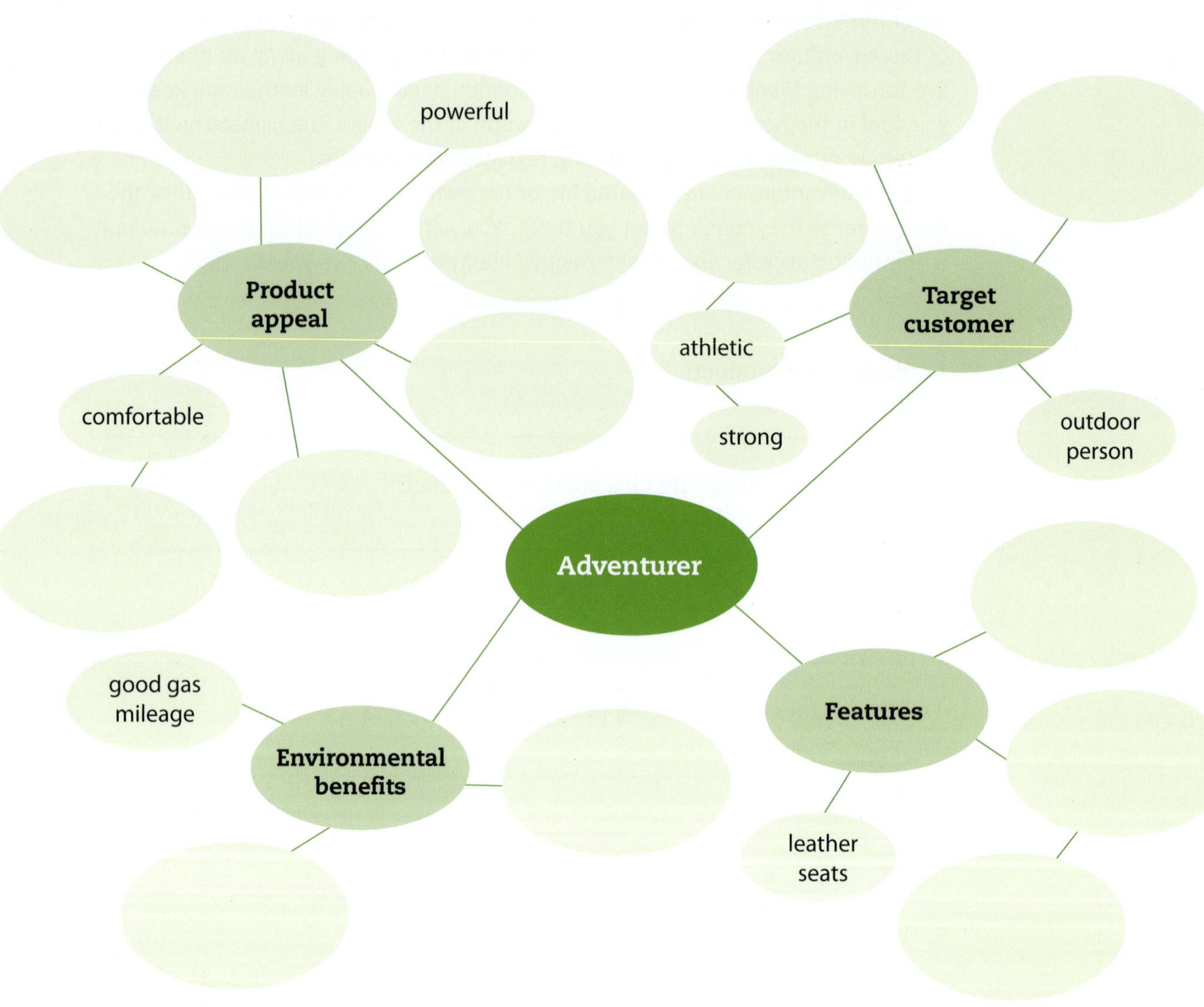

iQ ONLINE   **E.** Go online for more practice with descriptive essays.

A noun (a person, place, thing, or idea) is often introduced by an article. Different types of nouns can use different articles. Understanding the context in which a noun occurs will help you use articles correctly.

	Singular count noun	Plural count noun	Noncount noun
Indefinite article	*a* + consonant sound *an* + vowel sound	no article	no article
Definite article	*the*	*the*	*the*

Indefinite articles with nonspecific nouns

Use *a/an* or no article when a noun is not specifically identified or is unknown to the reader; for example, the first time you mention a noun.

> We were excited to have **a new car**. (This is the first reference to *a new car*. The reader does not know about it yet.)
>
> We bought **fish** for dinner. (No article is used with noncount nouns.)

You also use no article with plural count nouns or noncount nouns to refer to something in general.

> **Shoppers** can get a great deal of information from window displays.
>
> (*Shoppers* refers to any shopper, not a specific shopper.)

Definite articles with specific nouns

Use *the* when a noun is specifically identified. Both the reader and the writer know the noun because they share information about it. For example:

- The noun was already introduced.

> We were excited to have <u>a new car</u>, but **the car** we chose was terrible!
>
> (*A new car* was introduced earlier in the sentence.)

- The noun relates directly to something else that you introduced.

> Let's go to Ben's Diner. **The owners** are really friendly, and **the soup** is delicious.
>
> (The reader and writer both know that *the owners* refers to the owners of Ben's Diner, and *the soup* is served at Ben's Diner.)

- The noun is unique so the reader will know what you are referring to.

> **The Internet** has changed the way people look for homes.
>
> (There is only one Internet. It is unique.)
>
> **The government** should do more about false advertising.
>
> (You can assume the reader will know which government you are referring to.)

Tip for Success

Using *the* is not the only way to refer to a specific noun. You may also identify specific nouns with possessive adjectives (*my, your, their,* etc.), demonstrative adjectives (*this, that, these,* or *those*), or quantifiers (*two, many,* or *some*).

To:	Louis Rogers
From:	Felix Thompson
Subject:	Big news!

Hi Louis,

Sorry I haven't been in touch for a while, but I have __Ø__
 (1) big news. I got ____ (2) job that I told you about, so I'm selling
my house! You know that ____ (3) housing market is very tough
right now, but I'm happy because there is already ____ (4)
couple who are interested in my place. ____ (5) potential
buyers are coming over in two weeks. I want to stage ____ (6)
house so that everything looks perfect. I'm wondering if
you might be able to help me, so I thought I'd tell you what I'm planning.

This weekend, I'm going to clean ____ (7) house all over and repaint all ____ (8)
doors. I also bought ____ (9) awesome dining table to put in ____ (10) kitchen.
(I need some help picking it up!) Then I want to paint ____ (11) main bedroom—
probably in ____ (12) soft blue color. And when ____ (13) weather is nice, I want to
clean up ____ (14) yard and plant ____ (15) flowers.

Real estate agents always say that when ____ (16) buyers are looking at ____ (17)
houses, they want to feel like they already live there, so I know this will be
worth all ____ (18) effort.

Let me know if you can help me. Oh, and one other question. Do you
know where I can find ____ (19) good hardware store?

Felix

B. Go online for more practice with definite and indefinite articles.

C. Go online for the grammar expansion.

In this assignment, you are going to write an essay describing and selling features of a product, business, or service. As you prepare your essay, think about the Unit Question, "What makes you want to buy something?" Use information from Reading 1, Reading 2, the unit video, and your work in this unit to support your essay. Refer to the Self-Assessment checklist on page 60.

iQ ONLINE Go to the Online Writing Tutor for a writing model and alternate Unit Assignments.

PLAN AND WRITE

A. BRAINSTORM Follow these steps to help you organize your ideas.

1. Think of some products, businesses, and services that you have strong opinions about. These could be things like restaurants, stores, or products like new technology.

2. Answer these questions for each product, business, or service.
   a. How would you describe it? Think about descriptive language you can use.
   b. What are the main features or qualities of the product, business, or service?
   c. What do you like or dislike about the qualities or features?

3. Choose one product, business, or service that you would like to sell.

Writing Tip

You can use a **cluster diagram** to help you organize and develop your ideas. See page 56 for an example.

B. PLAN Follow these steps to plan your essay.

1. Choose two or three main features or qualities of the product, business, or service from question 2 in Activity A.

2. Brainstorm some descriptive language to give a clear mental picture of each feature or quality you selected.

3. Go to the Online Resources to download and complete the outline for your descriptive essay.

C. WRITE Use your **PLAN** notes to write your essay. Go to *iQ Online* to use the Online Writing Tutor.

1. Write your essay describing a product, business, or service. Be sure to include a thesis statement telling why it is your focus and body paragraphs with the specific features or qualities of your product, business, or service.

2. Look at the Self-Assessment checklist below to guide your writing.

REVISE AND EDIT

A. PEER REVIEW Read your partner's essay. Then go online and use the Peer Review worksheet. Discuss the review with your partner.

B. REWRITE Based on your partner's review, revise, and rewrite your essay.

C. EDIT Complete the Self-Assessment checklist as you prepare to write the final draft of your essay. Be prepared to hand in your work or discuss it in class.

SELF-ASSESSMENT		
Yes	No	
☐	☐	Does the thesis statement have a topic and controlling idea?
☐	☐	Does the essay use descriptive language to create a clear mental picture of the subject?
☐	☐	Are correct articles used?
☐	☐	Did you use collocations from the unit correctly?
☐	☐	Does the essay include vocabulary from the unit?
☐	☐	Did you check the essay for punctuation, spelling, and grammar?

D. REFLECT Go to the Online Discussion Board to discuss these questions.

1. What is something new you learned in this unit?

2. Look back at the Unit Question—What makes you want to buy something? Is your answer different now than when you started the unit? If yes, how is it different? Why?

TRACK YOUR SUCCESS

Circle the words and phrases you have learned in this unit.

Nouns

concept 🔑 AWL

individual 🔑 AWL

investment 🔑 AWL

negative 🔑 AWL

pedestrian

priority 🔑 AWL

residence AWL

Verbs

distinguish 🔑

evolve AWL

feature 🔑 AWL

liberate AWL

minimize AWL

promote 🔑 AWL

remove 🔑 AWL

tend 🔑

visualize AWL

Phrasal Verbs

allude to

focus on 🔑 AWL

Adjectives

neutral AWL

potential 🔑 AWL

sophisticated

urban 🔑

Adverb

mentally 🔑 AWL

Collocations

Adjective + Noun

full story

hard time

modern times

personal item

personal style

quick look

social rules

the old days

Verb + Noun

catch the eye

create a mood

give an impression

grab attention

make an impression

take a look

take pleasure

Preposition + Noun

at a time

in a hurry 🔑

in a way

in the field

in theory 🔑 AWL

on the market

over time

🔑 Oxford 3000™ words

AWL Academic Word List

Check (✓) the skills you learned. If you need more work on a skill, refer to the page(s) in parentheses.

READING	☐ I can highlight and annotate a text. (p. 42)
VOCABULARY	☐ I can recognize and use collocations with nouns. (p. 50)
WRITING	☐ I can write a descriptive essay. (p. 52)
GRAMMAR	☐ I can use definite and indefinite articles. (p. 57)
UNIT OBJECTIVE ▶▶▶▶	☐ I can gather information and ideas to write a descriptive essay about a product, business, or service.

READING ▶ making inferences
VOCABULARY ▶ prefixes and suffixes
WRITING ▶ writing a narrative and varying sentence patterns
GRAMMAR ▶ past perfect and past perfect continuous

UNIT QUESTION

What important lessons do we learn as children?

A Discuss these questions with your classmates.

1. What are some significant memories from your childhood?

2. What are some things that parents and their children disagree about?

3. Look at the photo. How do you think the children feel? What important lesson will they learn?

B Listen to *The Q Classroom* online. Then answer these questions.

1. What important lessons did Felix, Sophy, and Yuna learn as children? What is one lesson you learned?

2. What does Marcus say about what he learned from his parents? Sophy disagrees with Marcus. Who do you agree with? Why?

 **C** Go to the Online Discussion Board to discuss the Unit Question with your classmates.

UNIT OBJECTIVE ▶▶▶▶ Read a magazine article and an excerpt from a memoir and gather information and ideas to write a narrative essay about someone or something that influenced you.

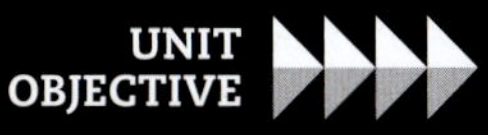

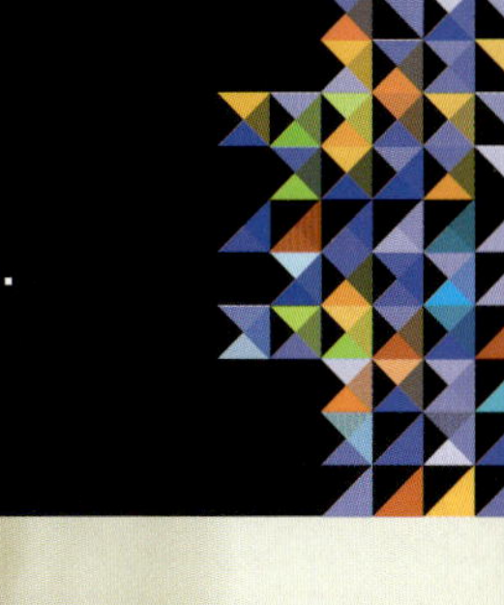

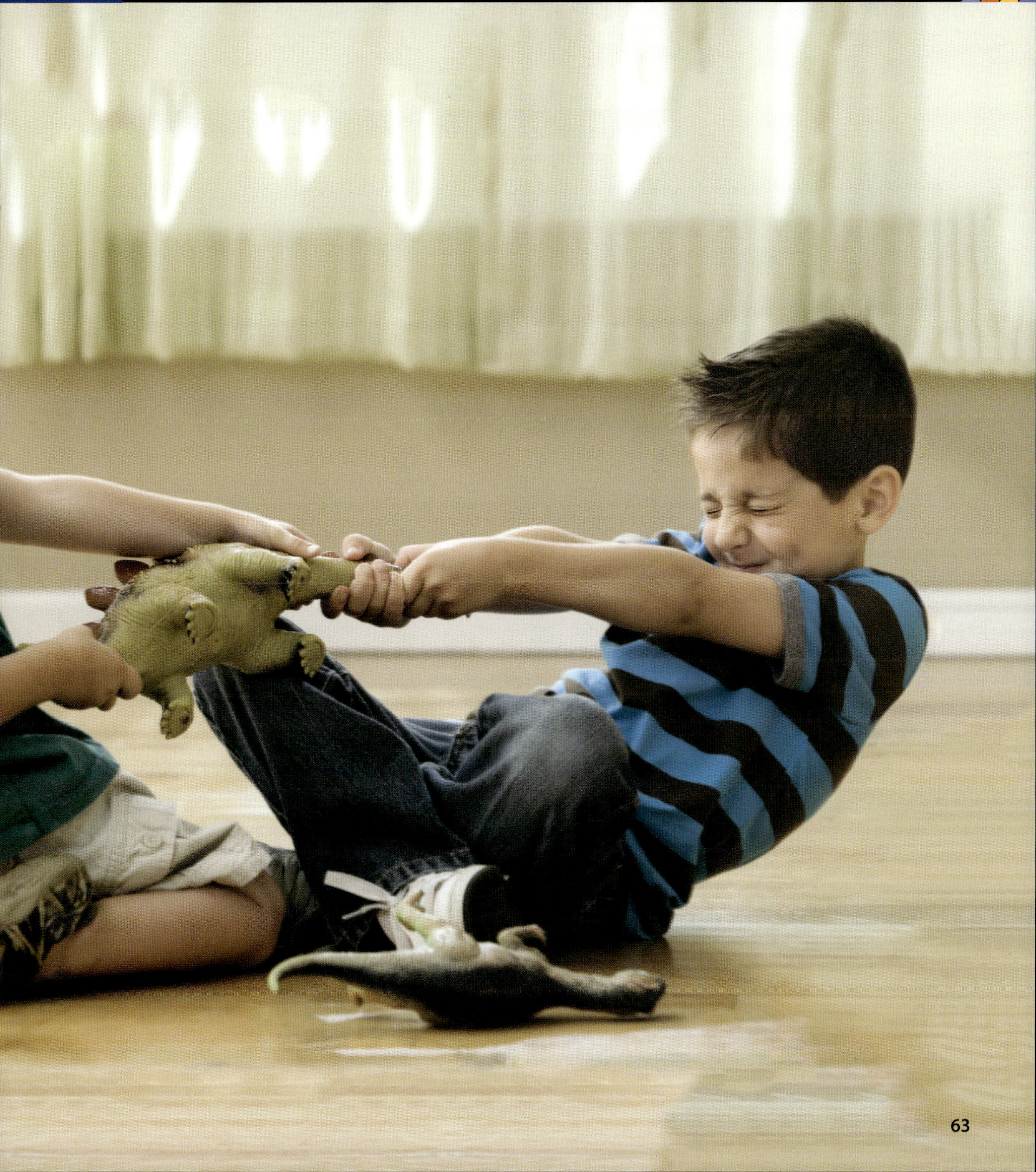

D Use the survey to interview a partner. Take notes on the answers.

		When you were a kid	Now
The basics	1.	What city did you grow up in?	Where do you live now?
	2.	What kind of child were you? Well-behaved? Fun-loving? Shy?	What are you like now?
Dreams and memories	3.	What did you want to be when you grew up?	What do you want to be now?
	4.	What is your best childhood memory?	What is your favorite recent memory?
School	5.	What subject did you like the most?	What's your favorite subject now?
	6.	How did you spend your summer break?	How do you like to spend vacations now?
Relationships	7.	What was your first best friend's name?	Is he/she still your friend?
	8.	Who were you closest to in your family?	Who are you closest to now?

E Look at the responses to the survey. Find three to five ways your partner has changed and discuss these questions.

1. In what way has your partner changed the most?

2. What else can your partner tell you about the changes?

READING

READING 1 | The Good Teen

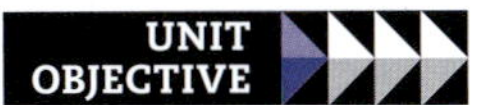

You are going to read a magazine article that examines commonly held beliefs about the behavior of teenagers. Use the article to gather information and ideas for your Unit Assignment.

PREVIEW THE READING

A. **PREVIEW** The word *adolescence* describes the period of growth and change from childhood to adulthood—often called *the teenage years*. Besides physical changes, what kinds of changes do people go through from childhood to adulthood? Discuss your ideas with a partner.

B. **QUICK WRITE** What are some things people believe about the behavior of teenagers? Think about their moods and emotions, their relationships with their families, and their relationships with their friends. Write for 5–10 minutes in response. Be sure to use this section for your Unit Assignment.

C. **VOCABULARY** Check (✓) the words you know. Then work with a partner to locate each word in the reading. Use clues to help define the words you don't know. Check your definitions in the dictionary.

accurately *(adv.)* 🔑	extracurricular *(adj.)*
assumption *(n.)*	innate *(adj.)*
colleague *(n.)* 🔑	nurture *(v.)*
competence *(n.)*	period *(n.)* 🔑
consistent with *(phr.)* 🔑	select *(v.)* 🔑
equipped with *(phr.)*	theoretically *(adv.)*

🔑 Oxford 3000™ words

D. Go online to listen and practice your pronunciation.

A. Read the article and gather information about the important lessons we learn as children.

The Good Teen

1   Eliza Parks is a high school senior. She gets good grades, is president of the senior class, and writes for the school newspaper. As a junior, she received her school's top prizes in English and history, and was **selected** to represent the school at a statewide speech contest. Not surprisingly, Eliza has been accepted at Yale University next year, where she has been awarded a scholarship. Even with all her **extracurricular** activities and academic commitments, Eliza makes time to be with her brother and her parents. Whenever possible, they eat dinner as a family, and often take trips together on weekends. Eliza also has a strong network of friends who her parents know well. "I talk with my parents very freely about my friends, my life, whatever," she says.

2   What is the secret to Eliza's happy adolescence? We often think of adolescence as a difficult **period**: the stereotypical[1] teenager makes poor decisions, hangs out with the wrong friends, or takes dangerous risks. Many parents often dread these years because they think their children will stop talking to them and refuse to follow their rules. However, recent research suggests that this common **assumption** about adolescence is often not true. Many teens not only survive these years, they thrive[2]. Instead of rebelling[3], many adopt the values of their parents. Instead of getting into trouble, they learn to work hard. Instead of forming negative relationships, they look for good role models and find supportive friends. In particular, teens **equipped with** specific skills and qualities may be better at avoiding the dangers others experience.

3   Dr. Richard Lerner, Director of the Institute for Applied Research in Youth Development at Tufts University, agrees that "most teens do not have a stormy adolescence." In order to discover how teens navigate these years happily and successfully, Lerner and his **colleagues** have conducted a long-range study of teens and their parents. This research, the 4-H Study of Positive Youth Development, examines how young people interact with others. It pays close attention to the activities they are involved in. It also looks at the adults who guide and support these children. The study identifies five interconnected characteristics for positive development in

---

[1] **stereotypical:** an image that people have of a type of person or thing which is often not true

[2] **thrive:** to become successful, strong, and healthy

[3] **rebelling:** fighting against or refusing to obey rules

adolescents, called the *Five Cs*: **competence**, confidence, connection, character, and caring. Researchers suggest that young people who have the Five Cs will also demonstrate a sixth C—contribution to self, family, community, and society. Teens with the Five Cs are more likely to become capable adults. And, **theoretically**, young people without the Five Cs would be at higher risk for a variety of social and personal problems.

4   How does Eliza fare[4] in terms of these characteristics? She has social and academic skills which allow her to excel in school (competence). Perhaps because of her talents, she has a good feeling about herself and her abilities (confidence). She has positive bonds with family, friends, and people at school (connection), and a good sense of right and wrong (character). And finally, Eliza cares about other people (caring). Her qualities and experience reflect all Five Cs. At least in Eliza's case, having the Five Cs **accurately** predicts her success.

5   But could it be that kids like Eliza are happier because they have fewer problems than others? That doesn't seem to be true. The 4-H Study has found that teens from any background can thrive. It doesn't matter if they are rich or poor, from the city or the country, living in a high-crime area or a low-crime area—anyone can do well with a little help. Researchers say that even adolescents with very serious problems can be successful if they are resilient. This means that even when they get knocked down by life, they can bounce back and recover quickly from the negative experience.

6   So, how do teens develop the Five Cs and become more resilient? Lerner's study found that families, schools, and communities are key[5]. "Quality time spent with teachers, parents, mentors, or in effective out-of-school programs put [young people] on a positive path to community contributions," he says.

According to Lerner, teens need opportunities that **nurture** positive interactions with adults, develop life skills (skills that will help them deal with the challenges of everyday life), and give them the chance to show leadership.

7   For parents, contact is critical. Although teens are starting to pull away, parents need to stay connected. One way is to participate in out-of-school activities. For example, kids and parents could volunteer to take care of a park or build a playground. But parents don't have to work on long-term projects to have an effect. Just spending time with teens can help. For example, one of the strongest predictors[6] of positive youth development was that a family ate dinner together on a regular basis. It is also important for parents to give teens time and space to explore their own interests and passions.

8   All these recommendations are **consistent with** the advice of psychologist Laurence Steinberg of Temple University. According to Steinberg, author of *The 10 Basic Principles of Good Parenting*, parents should be involved in their children's lives and give them plenty of love. In his book, Steinberg says that good parenting encourages "elements like honesty, empathy[7], self-reliance, kindness, cooperation, self-control, and cheerfulness." Sounds a lot like the Five Cs. Steinberg recognizes that for some people, good parenting is **innate**, but all parents can improve their skills through practice.

9   The message for parents is a good one. Your teenagers will not necessarily suffer and neither will you. Their connections to *both* friends and family will help them succeed during this period. But letting them have the one thing they really want—some independence—may actually help by giving them a sense of competence and control. During these years, parents need to find a balance between staying connected and letting go. This may be the best rule a parent can make.

---

[4] **fare:** to be successful or unsuccessful in a particular situation
[5] **key:** most important
[6] **predictors:** information that can show what will happen in the future
[7] **empathy:** the ability to understand another person's feelings

B. **VOCABULARY** Complete the sentences with the vocabulary from Reading 1.

accurately *(adv.)*	competence *(n.)*	extracurricular *(adj.)*	period *(n.)*
assumption *(n.)*	consistent with *(phr.)*	innate *(adj.)*	select *(v.)*
colleague *(n.)*	equipped with *(phr.)*	nurture *(v.)*	theoretically *(adv.)*

1. For our research project, my _________________ and I looked at the reasons that some teenagers do well in school.

2. We decided to conduct a second experiment, and we were pleased to see that the new results were _________________ the previous ones.

3. _________________, getting a college degree should help you get a good job.

4. I'll need more information in order to _________________ answer the question.

5. His _________________ activities include the school soccer team and the debate club.

6. You should carefully review the information in the guide before you _________________ your classes for the term.

7. University classrooms are _________________ a lot of technology to enhance students' learning opportunities.

8. The director said she was impressed with the _________________ Victor showed in his role as student council president.

9. Good parents will _________________ their children's dreams and help them realize their goals.

10. It's easy to make a judgment about someone based on a false _________________.

11. Even writers with _________________ talent need formal training, too.

12. We often think of the years between childhood and adulthood as a difficult _________________.

C. Go online for more practice with the vocabulary.

D. Answer these questions.

1. What assumption about adolescence does the research examine?

2. What are the Five Cs?

3. In what way is Eliza like other successful teens?

4. According to Dr. Lerner, what do teens need to develop the Five Cs?

5. According to Dr. Steinberg, what does good parenting encourage?

E. **Circle the correct answer. Then discuss your answers with a partner.**

1. What is the purpose of the first paragraph?
   a. It gives an example of the topic of the article.
   b. It gives a definition of the topic of the article.
   c. It gives a suggestion for a solution to a problem.

2. What is the main idea of paragraph 2?
   a. Eliza has a secret to being happy.
   b. People think that adolescents have lots of problems because they do.
   c. People think that adolescents have lots of problems, but they don't.

3. The 4-H Study of Positive Youth Development looked at ____.
   a. troubled adolescents and institutions that deal with them
   b. activities that successful teens are involved in
   c. how schools change their programs to deal with troubled teens

4. The purpose of paragraph 4 is to show ____.
   a. how Eliza's experiences and skills compare with the Five Cs
   b. that the Five Cs do not apply to Eliza
   c. how Eliza could do better if she knew about the Five Cs

5. How does being resilient help teens?
   a. It teaches leadership skills that they can use in later life.
   b. It helps them succeed in spite of problems.
   c. It allows them to get better more quickly when they are sick.

6. According to the article, ____.
   a. teens need to do things with supportive adults
   b. teens need their parents to work on long-term projects with them
   c. parents don't need to interact with their teenagers

7. The author probably included paragraph 8 ____.
   a. to show the opposite view by giving another expert's ideas
   b. to support his view by using another expert's ideas
   c. to question whether the 4-H Study was right

8. The audience for this reading is probably ____.
   a. teenagers   b. researchers   c. parents

F. Write *T* (true) or *F* (false) for each statement. Then correct each false statement to make it true. Write the paragraph number where you found information to support your answer.

____ 1. Eliza Parks has a good relationship with her parents. (paragraph ____)

____ 2. Many people assume that teens will make poor decisions. (paragraph ____)

____ 3. Lawrence Steinberg conducted the 4-H Study. (paragraph ____)

____ 4. The 4-H Study says that teens with the Five Cs are more likely to help in their communities. (paragraph ____)

____ 5. Eating dinner as a family is important to positive youth development. (paragraph ____)

____ 6. Steinberg thinks that parents can become better through practice. (paragraph ____)

____ 7. Parents should try to control their children during adolescence. (paragraph ____)

G. Go online to read *Siblings and Social Skills* and check your comprehension.

WRITE WHAT YOU THINK

A. Discuss these questions in a group.

1. Choose three of the activities in the box and discuss which of the Five Cs each one involves. (There will be more than one C for each activity.) Explain your answers.

coaching younger athletes	playing on a sports team	speaking in public
finding a career	reading to young children	

2. What other kinds of activities do you think help adolescents develop the traits that help them become responsible adults?

3. How can you relate the Five Cs to your childhood? Give an example from your experience in which your development was affected by one of these characteristics.

B. Choose one question and write a paragraph in response. Look back at your Quick Write on page 65 as you think about what you learned.

Writers don't usually state all their ideas directly. Usually, they expect the reader to **infer** some ideas that the information suggests. Making inferences about a text means that you use your knowledge to make a logical conclusion about the information that is given. Look at this excerpt from Reading 1.

> The 4-H Study has found that teens from any background can thrive. It doesn't matter if they are rich or poor, from the city or the country, living in a high-crime area or a low-crime area—anyone can do well with a little help.

In order to make these claims, the researchers had to do the right kind of research. So you can infer:

- They chose to research teens from many backgrounds.
- They also looked at the kind of help those teens received in order to be successful.

Making inferences helps you improve your comprehension and understand a text more deeply.

A. Read the paragraph from Reading 1. Check (✓) the statements that can be inferred from the text. Then compare your answers with a partner. Explain what information in the paragraph led to the inference.

Tip for Success

Your inferences should always depend on the author's words first and your experience second. Make sure your inferences are not contradicted by statements that are made later in the text.

> Eliza Parks is a high school senior. She gets good grades, is president of the senior class, and writes for the school newspaper. As a junior, she received her school's top prizes in English and history, and was selected to represent the school at a statewide speech contest. Not surprisingly, Eliza has been accepted at Yale University next year, where she has been awarded a scholarship. Even with all her extracurricular activities and academic commitments, Eliza makes time to be with her brother and her parents. Whenever possible, they eat dinner as a family, and often take trips together on weekends. Eliza also has a strong network of friends who her parents know well. "I talk with my parents very freely about my friends, my life, whatever," she says.

☐ 1. Eliza likes schoolwork.

☐ 2. Eliza is also very good at math.

☐ 3. Eliza speaks well in public.

☐ 4. Eliza succeeds at everything she tries.

☐ 5. Eliza's family does not have a lot of money.

☐ 6. Eliza is a very busy person.

☐ 7. Eliza enjoys spending time with her parents.

☐ 8. Eliza's mother is a good cook.

☐ 9. Eliza's parents help her choose her friends.

☐ 10. Eliza is a confident person.

B. Read the paragraph. Circle the answer(s) to each question. You may circle *a*, *b*, or both. Then compare your answers with a partner. Explain your answers.

> I have always had to struggle to get out of bed in the morning. When I was a young child, the problem wasn't so bad. Because I didn't want to miss anything that my older siblings were doing, I made myself get up. But as each one of them went away to college, I had less and less enthusiasm to get up in the mornings. After they were all gone, my father used to come to my bedroom door, knock, and say, "It's 6:00. Wake up and get out of bed." I would respond, "One or the other, Dad. One or the other."

1. What can you infer about the writer?
   a. The writer is an adult.
   b. The writer is male.

2. What can you infer about the writer's family?
   a. The writer had four older siblings.
   b. The writer was the youngest child.

3. What can you infer about the writer's problem?
   a. The writer still struggles to get out of bed.
   b. It was easier to get out of bed as a child than as a teenager.

4. What can you infer about the writer's father?
   a. He used to get up early.
   b. He was annoyed because the writer wouldn't get up.

5. What can you infer from the writer's response to the father?
   a. The writer has a good sense of humor.
   b. The writer would get up right away.

C. Go online for more practice making inferences.

READING 2 | Bird by Bird

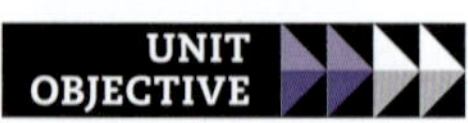

You are going to read an excerpt from author Anne Lamott's memoir, *Bird by Bird: Some Instructions on Writing and Life*. In it, she looks back at her childhood and the influence that her father had on her. Use the excerpt to gather information and ideas for your Unit Assignment.

PREVIEW THE READING

A. PREVIEW Skim the excerpt. Check (✓) the correct statement.

    ☐ Anne Lamott decided to become a writer because of her father.

    ☐ Despite her family's wishes, Anne Lamott decided to become a writer.

B. QUICK WRITE Who influenced you most as a child? Write for 5–10 minutes in response. Be sure to use this section for your Unit Assignment.

C. VOCABULARY Check (✓) the words you know. Use a dictionary to define any new or unknown words. Then discuss how the words will relate to the unit with a partner.

capture (v.) 🔑	impassioned (adj.)	refuge (n.)
creative (adj.) 🔑	motivate (v.)	resentful (adj.)
episode (n.)	profound (adj.)	significance (n.)
exaggerate (v.) 🔑	rely on (phr. v.) 🔑	suspect (v.) 🔑

🔑 Oxford 3000™ words

D. Go online to listen and practice your pronunciation.

WORK WITH THE READING

A. Read the excerpt and gather information about the important lessons we learn as children.

BIRD BY BIRD

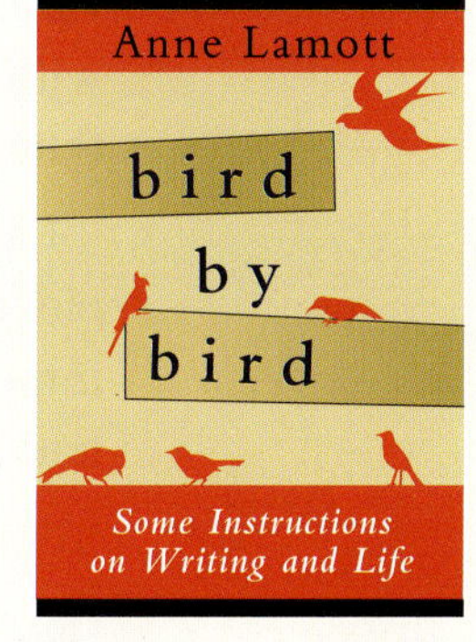

1   Every morning, no matter how late he had been up, my father rose at 5:30, went to his study, wrote for a couple of hours, made us all breakfast, read the paper with my mother, and then went back to work for the rest of the morning. Many years passed before I realized that he did this by choice, for a living, and that he was not unemployed or mentally ill. I wanted him to have a regular job where he put on a necktie and went off somewhere with the other fathers and sat in a little office. . . . But the idea of spending entire days in someone else's office doing someone else's work did not suit my father's soul. I think it would have killed him. He did end up dying rather early, in his mid-fifties, but at least he had lived on his own terms.

2   So I grew up around this man who sat at his desk in the study all day and wrote books and articles about the places and people he had seen and known. He read a lot of poetry. Sometimes he traveled. He could go anyplace he wanted with a sense of purpose. One of the gifts of being a writer is that it gives you an excuse to do things, to go places and explore. Another is that writing **motivates** you to look closely at life, at life as it lurches by[1] and tramps around[2].

3   Writing taught my father to pay attention; my father in turn taught other people to pay attention and then to write down their thoughts and observations. His students were the prisoners at San Quentin[3] who took part in the creative-writing program. But he taught me, too, mostly by example. He taught the prisoners and me to put a little bit down on paper every day, and to read all the great books we could get our hands on. He taught us to read poetry. He taught us to be bold and original and to let ourselves make mistakes. . . . But while he helped the prisoners and me to discover that we had a lot of feelings and observations and memories and dreams and opinions we wanted to share, we all ended up just the tiniest bit **resentful** when we found the one fly in the ointment[4]: that at some point we had to actually sit down and write.

4   I believe writing was easier for me than for the prisoners because I was still a child. But I always found it hard. I started writing when I was seven or eight. I was very shy and strange-looking, loved reading above everything else, weighed about forty pounds at the time, and was so tense that I walked around with my shoulders up to my ears. I saw a video once of a celebration I went to in the first grade, with all these cute little boys and girls playing together like puppies, and all of a sudden I scuttled across the screen like Prufrock's crab[5]. I was very clearly the one who was going to grow up to . . . keep dozens and dozens of cats. Instead, I got funny. I walked in a strange way: I think I was trying to plug my ears with my shoulders, but they wouldn't quite reach. So first I got funny and then I started to write, although I did not always write funny things.

5   I started writing a lot in high school: journals, **impassioned** antiwar pieces, parodies of the writers I loved. And I began to notice something important. The other kids always wanted me to tell them stories of what had happened, even—or especially—when they had been there. Blowups[6]

---

[1] **lurches by:** makes a sudden, unsteady movement forward or sideways
[2] **tramps around:** travels or wanders on foot
[3] **San Quentin:** a state prison in California
[4] **fly in the ointment:** something that spoils the enjoyment
[5] **Prufrock's crab:** a shy, timid character that appears in a well-known poem by T. S. Eliot
[6] **blowup:** a fight or conflict

in the classroom or on the school yard, scenes involving their parents that we had witnessed—I could make the story happen. I could make it vivid and funny, and even **exaggerate** some of it so that the event became almost mythical, and the people involved seemed larger, and there was a sense of larger **significance**, of meaning.

6   I'm sure my father was the person **on** whom his friends **relied** to tell their stories, in school and college. I know for sure that he was later, in the town where he was raising his children. He could take major events or small **episodes** from daily life and shade or exaggerate things in such a way as to **capture** their shape and substance, capture what life felt like in the society in which he and his friends lived and worked. . . . People looked to him to put into words what was going on.

7   I **suspect** that he was a child who thought differently than his peers, who may have had serious conversations with grown-ups, who as a young person, like me, accepted being alone quite a lot. I think that this sort of person often becomes either a writer or a career criminal. Throughout my childhood I believed that what I thought about was different from what other kids thought about. It was not necessarily more **profound**, but there was a struggle going on inside me to find some sort of **creative** or spiritual or aesthetic way of seeing the world and organizing it in my head. I read more than other kids; I luxuriated in books. Books were my **refuge**. I sat in corners with my little finger hooked over my bottom lip, reading, in a trance[7], lost in the places and time to which books took me. And there was a moment during my junior year in high school when I began to believe that I could do what other writers were doing. I came to believe that I might be able to put a pencil in my hand and make something special happen.

8   Then I wrote some terrible, terrible stories.

[7] **trance:** a condition in which you don't notice what is going on around you

---

B. VOCABULARY Complete the sentences with the vocabulary from Reading 2.

capture *(v.)*	exaggerate *(v.)*	profound *(adj.)*	resentful *(adj.)*
creative *(adj.)*	impassioned *(adj.)*	rely on *(phr. v.)*	significance *(n.)*
episode *(n.)*	motivate *(v.)*	refuge *(n.)*	suspect *(v.)*

1. Studying a new language can _______________ a person to travel.

2. My friends _______________ their stories so much it's hard to know which parts are true.

3. My brother speaks Italian very well, so whenever we go to Italy,

   I ________________ him to translate.

4. The writer used descriptive words to ____________ the mood of the place.

5. Many of the things my parents told me as a child seemed unimportant at

   the time, but I now realize the ____________________ of their words.

6. My aunt is a great storyteller. She can describe a simple

   ____________________ from the past in a really exciting way.

7. As the storm got worse, they had to find ____________________.

8. I ________________ that my friends are planning to surprise me,

   but I'm not really sure.

9. Marcos was furious about the article in the newspaper, and he

   wrote a(n) ________________ letter in response.

10. Ben should study geography. He's always interested in having

    ____________________ discussions about the environment.

11. I have a hard time coming up with ideas. I wish I were more ____________.

12. Ivan was ________________ because he wasn't allowed to play in

    the soccer game.

iQ ONLINE　**C. Go online for more practice with the vocabulary.**

**D. Each of these sentences gives the main idea of a paragraph in the reading.
Write the correct paragraph number (1–7) next to each sentence.**

____ a.　Her father taught his students how to write: for instance, to write a little
every day, to read great books, and not to be afraid of making mistakes.

____ b.　Writing gave her father a reason to explore things and motivated him
to look at life closely.

____ c.　In high school, she discovered that her classmates really liked stories
about things that had happened when they were there.

____ d.　Because she had a different way of thinking about things, she started
to believe that she could be a writer.

_____ e.   Her father had made the choice to work at home and be a writer.

_____ f.   Because she was nervous and shy, she learned to be funny and
           started writing.

_____ g.   Her father wrote about major events and small episodes from daily life
           in a way that expressed the atmosphere or feeling of the place and time.

E. **Answer the questions about Anne Lamott. Write the paragraph number
where you found the information for your answer.**

1. What do you think Lamott means by "life as it lurches by and tramps
   around"?

2. How does she describe herself as a child?

3. What is her purpose in describing herself as a child?

4. Why did the other kids in high school want her to tell them stories of what
   happened even when they were there?

5. Why does she call books her refuge?

F. **Anne Lamott writes about both her father and herself as storytellers.
Find a sentence in the reading that describes how each of them told
stories. Write the paragraph number and highlight the sentence.**

Anne Lamott: Paragraph _____   Her father: Paragraph _____

G. **Find these sentences in the excerpt. What can you infer from each
sentence? Circle the best answer. Then explain your answer to a partner.**

1. **Paragraph 1:** "I wanted him to have a regular job where he put on a necktie
   and went off somewhere with the other fathers and sat in a little office."
   a. The author wanted her father to spend more time out of the house.
   b. The author wanted her father to have a more "normal" job.

2. **Paragraph 2:** "Sometimes he traveled. He could go anyplace he wanted
   with a sense of purpose."
   a. When he traveled, he was thinking about how he could write about it.
   b. Because he worked at home, his schedule allowed him time to travel a lot.

3. **Paragraph 3:** ". . . we all ended up just the tiniest bit resentful when we
   found the one fly in the ointment: that at some point we had to actually
   sit down and write."
   a. The author thinks her father gave them too many writing assignments.
   b. The author thinks writing down your ideas is difficult.

4. **Paragraph 7:** "I suspect that he was a child who thought differently than his peers, who may have had serious conversations with grown-ups, who as a young person, like me, accepted being alone quite a lot."

   a. The author thinks that she and her father were very similar as children.

   b. The author thinks her father should have been more outgoing as a child.

WRITE WHAT YOU THINK

A. Discuss the questions in a group. Look back at your Quick Write on page 73 as you think about what you learned.

1. Think about a profession you are familiar with or interested in. What qualities does a person in that profession have or need to have?

2. Think about a person who influenced you as a child or teenager. How did that person affect who you are today?

B. Before you watch the video, discuss the questions in a group.

1. Have you ever wanted to quit doing an activity you originally liked? What did you do?

2. Should children be allowed to quit doing after-school activities, like playing on a soccer team or ice skating? Why or why not?

C. Go online to watch the video about children who want to quit doing an activity. Then check your comprehension.

couch potato *(n.)* a person who spends a lot of time sitting and watching television

instill *(v.)* to make someone feel a particular way over time

rule of thumb *(n.)* a practical method of measuring something, usually based on past experience

stamina *(n.)* physical or mental strength that enables you to do something for long periods

D. Think about the unit video, Reading 1, and Reading 2 as you discuss the questions. Then choose one question and write a paragraph in response.

1. Reading 1 describes the five Cs that help adolescents move successfully into adulthood. Which of the five Cs does the author of Reading 2 display?

2. Did you ever want to quit an activity like a sports team when you were a child? How did quitting or not quitting affect who you are now?

A **prefix** is a group of letters that comes at the beginning of a word. When you add a prefix to a word, it usually changes the word's meaning. Study the chart of prefixes from Readings 1 and 2 and other common examples.

Prefix	Meaning	Example
anti-	against	antiwar
co-	together	cooperation
extra-	more	extracurricular
in-	not	independence
inter-	go between	interact
mid-	middle	mid-fifties
mis-	incorrect, badly	misunderstanding
re-	again	reread

A **suffix** is a group of letters that comes at the end of a word. When you add a suffix to a word, it usually changes the part of speech of that word. For example, adding the suffix *-tion* to the verb *inform* makes it the noun *information*. Study the chart of suffixes from Readings 1 and 2.

Suffixes that form nouns	-ence / -ance	competence, significance
	-tion	assumption, connection
Suffixes that form adjectives	-ent / -ant	consistent, important
	-ful	resentful, successful
Suffixes that form verbs	-ate	exaggerate, motivate
	-ize	organize, realize

A. Complete the word in each sentence with the correct prefix from the Vocabulary Skill box above. Then check your answers in the dictionary.

1. He _______ pronounced the word, so she didn't understand what he had said.

2. They were both _______ ordinary students. They excelled at school and were talented in sports and poetry as well.

3. Many parts of the brain are _______ connected. They work together to enable the brain's many functions.

4. His job required that he _______ locate often, so he had lived in many places.

5. Terry knew she wasn't ready for _______ term exams, but she hoped she'd do better on the final.

6. People assumed Jin was _______ social because he rarely spoke with other children.

7. Some siblings have to learn to _______ exist peacefully together.

8. We're going to have a(n) _______ formal gathering tonight. Come by if you want.

B. Read each word. Check (✓) the correct part of speech. Use information from the Vocabulary Skill box on page 79 to help you. Then check your answers in the dictionary.

	Noun	Adjective	Verb
1. recognize	☐	☐	☐
2. reliance	☐	☐	☐
3. peaceful	☐	☐	☐
4. demonstrate	☐	☐	☐
5. resilient	☐	☐	☐
6. contribution	☐	☐	☐
7. confidence	☐	☐	☐
8. significant	☐	☐	☐
9. substance	☐	☐	☐
10. navigate	☐	☐	☐
11. contribution	☐	☐	☐
12. cheerful	☐	☐	☐

C. Choose five words from Activity B. Write a sentence for each.

D. Go online for more practice with prefixes and suffixes.

WRITING

 At the end of this unit, you will write a narrative essay about someone or something that influenced you. This essay will include specific information from the readings, the unit video, and your own ideas.

Writing Skill — Writing a narrative essay and varying sentence patterns

A **narrative essay** tells a story about a personal experience, event, or memory.

Organization

- The **introduction** sets the scene for the reader. It should give information about the people, place, and time, and should create interest in the story. The introduction may include a **thesis statement** that tells why the story is important or memorable.
- There can be one or more **body paragraphs**. These tell the main events or actions of the story. They are usually in the order in which the events happened. They may also include important or interesting details to support the ideas in the main event.
- The **conclusion** gives the outcome or result of the actions in the story. It often tells what the writer learned from the experience.

Expressing the order of events

In a narrative essay, you use **time words** and **time clauses** to explain when the events happened in the story and the order of events.

> **Prepositions: in** 1978, **on** June 5, **before/after** class, **for** five years
>
> **Time expressions:** a week **ago**, **last** month, **earlier** this year, the week **before**, an hour **later**, the **next** day
>
> **Time clauses: after** we spoke, **before** I ate, **as** they were leaving, **when** we met

Varying sentence patterns

Varying sentence patterns in your writing will help the reader maintain interest and focus on important information. Here are some ways to add variety to your writing.

- Shorter sentences emphasize or stress one important point.
- Longer sentences combine closely related ideas. Longer sentences can be made by using conjunctions, subordinators, or relative clauses to combine shorter sentences.

> **Shorter:** There was a sudden noise.
>
> **Longer (with conjunction):** Then a cat jumped out of the bushes **and** ran up the path.
>
> **Longer (with subordinator): Even though** it was only a cat, my heart started beating faster.
>
> **Longer (with relative clause):** The next noise **that I heard** was definitely not a cat.

A. Brainstorm ideas for a narrative essay.

1. Draw a timeline of four or five events that you remember from your childhood. Put on your timeline how old you were and a short phrase indicating what happened.

Example:

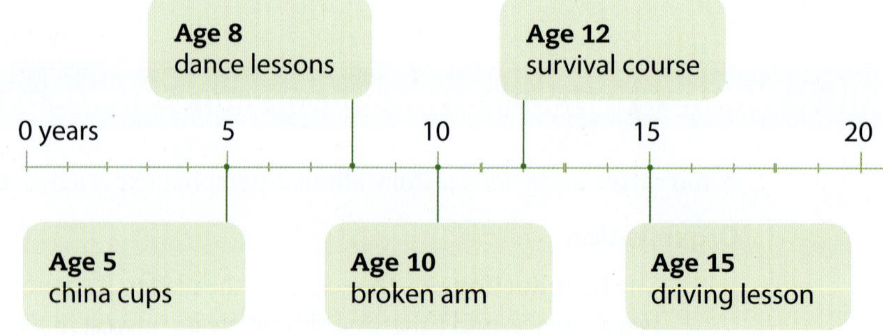

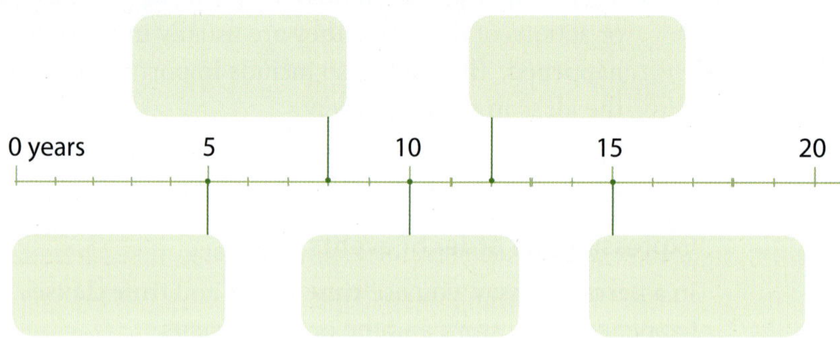

2. Choose one of the events on your timeline and answer these questions.

a. What happened?

____

b. Who was with you?

____

c. Where were you?

____

d. When did it happen?

____

e. What did you learn?

____

My Mother's China Cups

When I think about my mother, one thing I remember is her collection of china cups and saucers. She had collected them throughout her life, and they were very important to her. They were displayed on shelves in our kitchen. Some of them were quite old; some she had gotten from faraway places. And each one had a special memory for her.

From a very young age, I always wanted to take down those beautiful cups and wash them. It was my chance to see them up close. My mother never really wanted to let me do it. She knew the cups were fragile and I could easily break them. But sometimes I begged until she let me take them down and clean them.

My earliest memory of this was when I was five. I pulled a chair near the kitchen table and took down the small cups. I started with my favorites: the very old blue and white one that had belonged to my great-grandmother and the one from Japan with exotic buildings on it. I moved them all, one by one, to the kitchen counter. After I had put them on the counter, I moved my chair to the sink, filled the sink with soapy water, and began to wash the tiny cups.

I had only washed a few when the beautiful blue and white cup slipped from my small hands and fell back into the sink. The handle broke off. My mother's special cup was ruined, and I was sure she would be angry. I cried and waited for quite a while before I could find the courage to tell her. My mother, who was probably upset, only smiled and said we would glue it back together. I happily finished washing the precious cups. When I had cleaned and dried them all, we carefully placed them back on the shelves. Then my mother glued the handle back on the broken cup before we set it back in its place, too.

I washed those cups many times as a child, and almost every time, I broke one. By the time I was grown, several showed the signs of my efforts. I am an adult now and my mother is gone, but I will always remember that she cared more about encouraging me than about her valuable cups. Now, as a mother myself, I understand the patience it took to allow me to handle her precious things. I try to demonstrate that same level of caring to my own children.

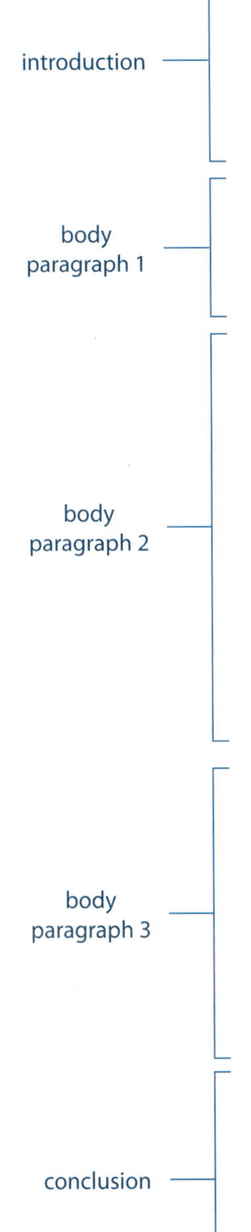

1. Who are the people in the narrative?

   ____

2. Where does the action take place?

   ____

3. When does the action take place?

   ____

When writing a narrative, use details and descriptive language to make the story come alive for the reader. See the Writing Skill on page 52 for more information.

C. Complete the outline of the essay. You do not have to use the writer's exact words.

I. Introductory ideas: _______________________________

   ____

II. Body paragraph 1: Main event in story

   When I was a child, I always wanted to wash my mother's china cups.

   A. Important or interesting detail: ___________________

   ____

   B. Important or interesting detail: ___________________

   ____

III. Body paragraph 2: Main event in story

   ____

   A. Important or interesting detail: _I started with my favorites—

   the old blue and white one and the one from Japan._

   B. Important or interesting detail: ___________________

   ____

IV. Body paragraph 3: Main event in story

   ____

   A. Important or interesting detail: ___________________

   ____

   B. Important or interesting detail: _My mother glued the handle on

   the cup before we put it back on the shelf._

V. Conclusion (what I learned): ___________________

   ____

D. **Look at body paragraph 3 of "My Mother's China Cups" on page 83. Circle the conjunctions. Underline the subordinators. Put a star (*) next to the relative clause. Then answer these questions.**

1. Write the shortest sentence here. ___________________________________

2. How many conjunctions did you find? ____

3. How many subordinators? ____

4. The relative clause has commas around it. Who does the relative clause

   describe? ___________________________

E. **Work with a partner to rewrite the paragraph below. Vary the sentence patterns by keeping some shorter sentences and by using conjunctions, subordinators, and relative clauses to make longer sentences.**

The toughest weekend of my life was also one of the best. I was 12. My father and I attended a short survival course. I will never forget it. I woke up early on a Saturday morning. It was still dark. I wanted to go back to sleep. My father was wide awake. My father was excited about the day ahead. We ate a quick breakfast. We drove to the school at the edge of the desert. We arrived at 7 a.m. The desert was already hot. I felt nervous. I didn't want to show it. The other students arrived. One was a boy. He was about my age. He was with his father, too. The instructor came out to greet us.

Example: The toughest weekend of my life was also one of the best. When I was 12, my father and I attended a short survival course that I will never forget.

F. **Go back to your paragraph from Activity E. Circle the conjunctions. Underline the subordinators. Put a star (*) next to the relative clauses. Then answer these questions.**

1. How many short sentences do you have? ____

2. How many sentences have conjunctions? ____

3. How many sentences have subordinators? ____

4. How many sentences have relative clauses? ____

G. **Read the rest of the essay from Activity E.**

The instructor—a tall, athletic man—looked at us seriously. "You are going to learn about survival," he said. "This may be the most challenging and rewarding weekend of your life." I looked at my father. I wasn't sure that I wanted to continue, but he was still very excited. "You will learn how to do such things as find food, find shelter, and keep warm. I won't tell you that it is going to be easy. In fact, it won't be. However, at the end of the weekend, I hope you'll think that it was worth the effort."

We set out with only our water bottles and knives. We hiked through the desert for miles in the hot sun. I was afraid that we would run out of water, but our guide said that we would be fine as long as we didn't waste any. Along the way, we looked for food. We found an edible plant that people call a barrel cactus. We also caught a lizard that people can boil and eat, but no one wanted to. We were hungry and tired when the instructor had us stop near some flowering cactus. We ate the flowers, which tasted OK, and we rested in the shade of some large rocks.

I don't remember much about the rest of the first day, but I do remember that the air got cold quickly when the sun set, and I was happy to sit close to my father, near the fire that we had helped build. I looked up at the stars and smiled. They were so beautiful, out away from the city. I looked up at my father and saw his face more peaceful than I could remember ever seeing it before.

It was a tough weekend, but I am glad we went. I learned about the desert and how to survive in it, but more importantly, I learned about myself and my father. We had shared a difficult time in the desert, and we grew closer because of it. Long afterward, whenever we saw the stars, one or the other would say, "Remember that night in the desert?" and we would both smile.

Choose one of the paragraphs in the essay. Circle the conjunctions. Underline the subordinators. Put a star (*) next to the relative clauses.

H. Go online for more practice with narrative essays and varying sentence patterns.

Grammar   Past perfect and past perfect continuous

Order of events in the past

The **past perfect** shows that one event happened before another event in the past. The past perfect expresses the earlier event. The simple past is often used to express the later event. The past perfect often gives background information about events or situations. It has the same form for all subjects: subject + *had* (+ *not*) + past participle.

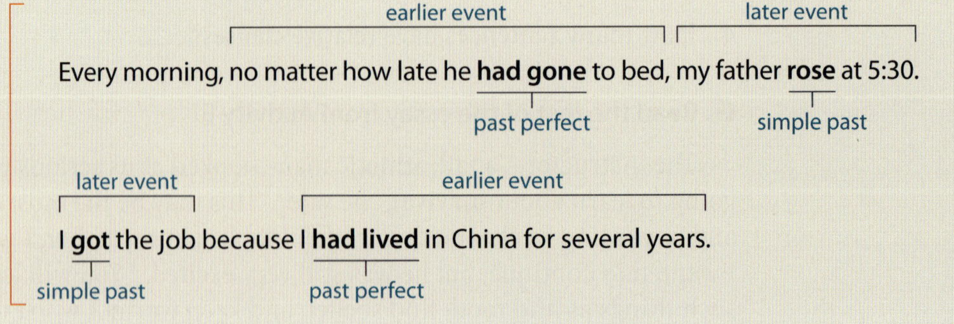

Past perfect with past time clauses

The past perfect is often used in sentences with **past time clauses**. A past time clause usually begins with a subordinator such as *when, until,* or *by the time.* Notice the use of a comma when the past time clause comes first.

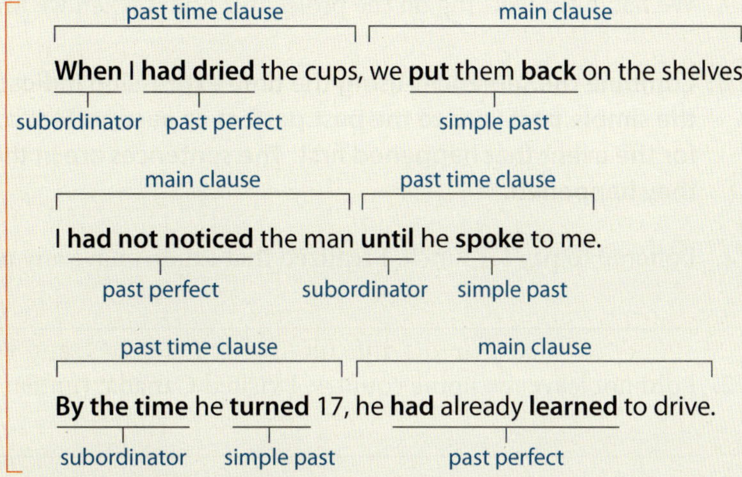

Past perfect continuous

The **past perfect continuous** is used for actions that began in the past and continued up to another past event or state in the past. It is often used with *for* to indicate how long a situation lasted. Like the past perfect, it often gives background information. The past perfect continuous is *had + been + verb + -ing.*

> I **had been living** there for six months when the Smiths moved next door.
> She **had been writing** stories for many years when her first story was published.
> When she finally arrived, **he'd been waiting** for her for two hours.

A. Read the sentences. Underline the past perfect and past perfect continuous verbs and circle the simple past verbs in each example. Label the verbs *1* for the earlier event and *2* for the later event.

1. My mother had a collection of very small china cups and saucers.

   She had collected them throughout her life.

2. I had only washed a few when the beautiful blue and white cup slipped

   from my small hands.

3. I had forgotten to call my brother, so he was angry with me.

4. She had thought seriously about studying medicine, but in the end

   she decided to study business.

5. Until he got an internship at a big ad agency, he hadn't been interested in working in advertising.

6. I didn't answer the man because I hadn't heard him clearly.

7. We had been working on the project for hours when we finally finished it.

B. **Combine the sentences using the time expression indicated. Change the simple past verb to the past perfect or past perfect continuous for the event that happened first. The sentences are in the order that they happened.**

I didn't have any money.

1. I offered to pay for lunch. I realized that I didn't have any money. (when)

   ____

2. I did not leave my home country. I visited Canada. (until)

   ____

3. He already finished reading the book. He watched the DVD. (when)

   ____

4. They recalled important events from their past. The students wrote stories about their memories of childhood. (after)

   ____

   ____

5. I had lunch. She arrived at the restaurant. (by the time)

   ____

6. She was studying English. She moved to the United States. (when)

   ____

iQ ONLINE **C.** **Go online for more practice with the past perfect and past perfect continuous.**

D. **Go online for the grammar expansion.**

Unit Assignment — Write a narrative essay

In this assignment, you are going to write a narrative essay about someone or something that influenced you when you were younger. As you prepare your essay, think about the Unit Question, "What important lessons do we learn as children?" Use information from Reading 1, Reading 2, the unit video, and your work in this unit to support your essay. Refer to the Self-Assessment checklist on page 90.

iQ ONLINE Go to the Online Writing Tutor for a writing model and alternate Unit Assignments.

PLAN AND WRITE

A. BRAINSTORM Follow these steps to help you organize your ideas.

1. Write down the names of some people or things that influenced you when you were younger.

Tip for Success

To help you remember all the details of your memory, ask and answer the six *wh-*questions: *who, what, where, when, why,* and *how.*

2. Think about memories associated with those people or things. Write notes about the memories and specific details such as people, times, and places.

People	Memories	Details
My older brother	The time I fell off my bike when we were kids	I was 6. We were in Greenway Park. I cut my head. We went to see Dr. Garcia.

Things	Memories	Details
Greenwich Elementary School	My first day of school	I was lost on my first day. Mrs. Lu found me in the school playground. She took me back to class.

B. PLAN Follow these steps to plan your essay.

1. Choose one of the people or things from Activity A to write about.

2. Circle the most interesting memories and the most important details.

3. Go to the Online Resources to download and complete the outline for your narrative essay.

C. **WRITE** Use your **PLAN** notes to write your essay. Go to *iQ Online* to use the Online Writing Tutor.

1. To clearly express the order of the events, use time words and time clauses, the past perfect and past perfect continuous, and other past verb forms.

2. Look at the Self-Assessment checklist below to guide your writing.

REVISE AND EDIT

A. **PEER REVIEW** Read your partner's essay. Then go online and use the Peer Review worksheet. Discuss the review with your partner.

B. **REVISE** Based on your partner's review, revise, and rewrite your essay.

C. **EDIT** Complete the Self-Assessment checklist as you prepare to write the final draft of your essay. Be prepared to hand in your work or discuss it in class.

Yes	No	SELF-ASSESSMENT
☐	☐	Does the introduction tell why the story is important?
☐	☐	Are the events in the order in which they happened?
☐	☐	Does the conclusion tell why the memory is important today?
☐	☐	Are time words and time clauses used to clearly express the order of the events?
☐	☐	Are the past perfect and past perfect continuous used appropriately to give background for other past events or situations?
☐	☐	Does the essay include vocabulary from the unit?
☐	☐	Did you check the essay for punctuation, spelling, and grammar?

D. **REFLECT** Go to the Online Discussion Board to discuss these questions.

1. What is something new you learned in this unit?

2. Look back at the Unit Question—What important lessons do we learn as children? Is your answer different now than when you started the unit? If yes, how is it different? Why?

TRACK YOUR SUCCESS

Circle the words and phrases you have learned in this unit.

Nouns
assumption AWL
colleague 🔑 AWL
competence
episode
refuge
period 🔑 AWL
significance AWL

Verbs
capture 🔑
exaggerate 🔑
motivate AWL
nurture
select 🔑 AWL
suspect 🔑

Phrasal Verb
rely on 🔑 AWL

Adjectives
creative 🔑 AWL
extracurricular
impassioned
innate
profound
resentful

Adverbs
accurately 🔑 AWL
theoretically AWL

Phrases
consistent with 🔑 AWL
equipped with AWL

Prefixes
anti- 🔑
co-
extra-
in-
inter-
mid-
mis-
re- 🔑

Suffixes
-ate
-ence / -ance
-ent / -ant
-ful
-ize
-tion

🔑 Oxford 3000™ words
AWL Academic Word List

Check (✓) the skills you learned. If you need more work on a skill, refer to the page(s) in parentheses.

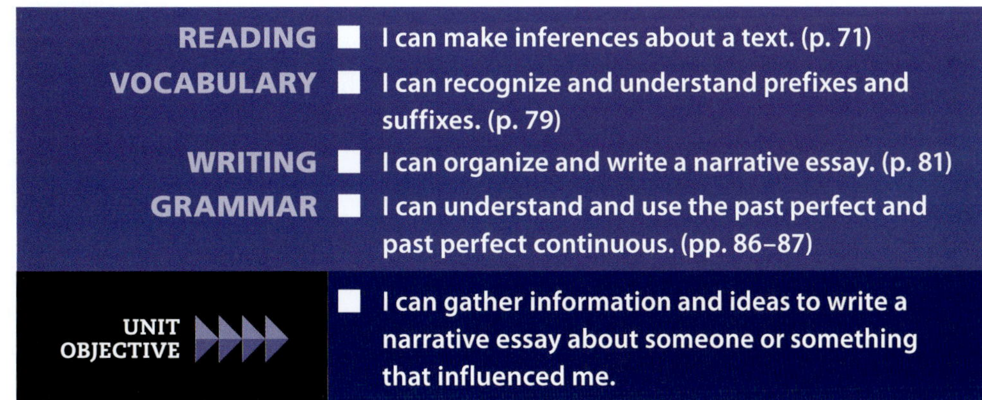

UNIT QUESTION

How important is it to write by hand?

A Discuss these questions with your classmates.

1. Do you like to write by hand? Why?

2. Why is it important to preserve the skill of writing?

3. Look at the photo. Why are these people writing by hand? Why might this be important to them?

B Listen to *The Q Classroom* online. Then answer these questions.

1. What are Marcus's reasons for not writing by hand?

2. What are reasons the other students give for writing by hand? Who do you agree with? Why?

 **C** Go to the Online Discussion Board to discuss the Unit Question with your classmates.

UNIT OBJECTIVE Read an article from an education journal and a biography and gather information and ideas to write an essay comparing and contrasting two forms of writing.

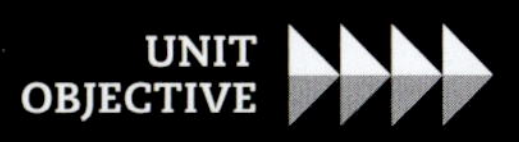

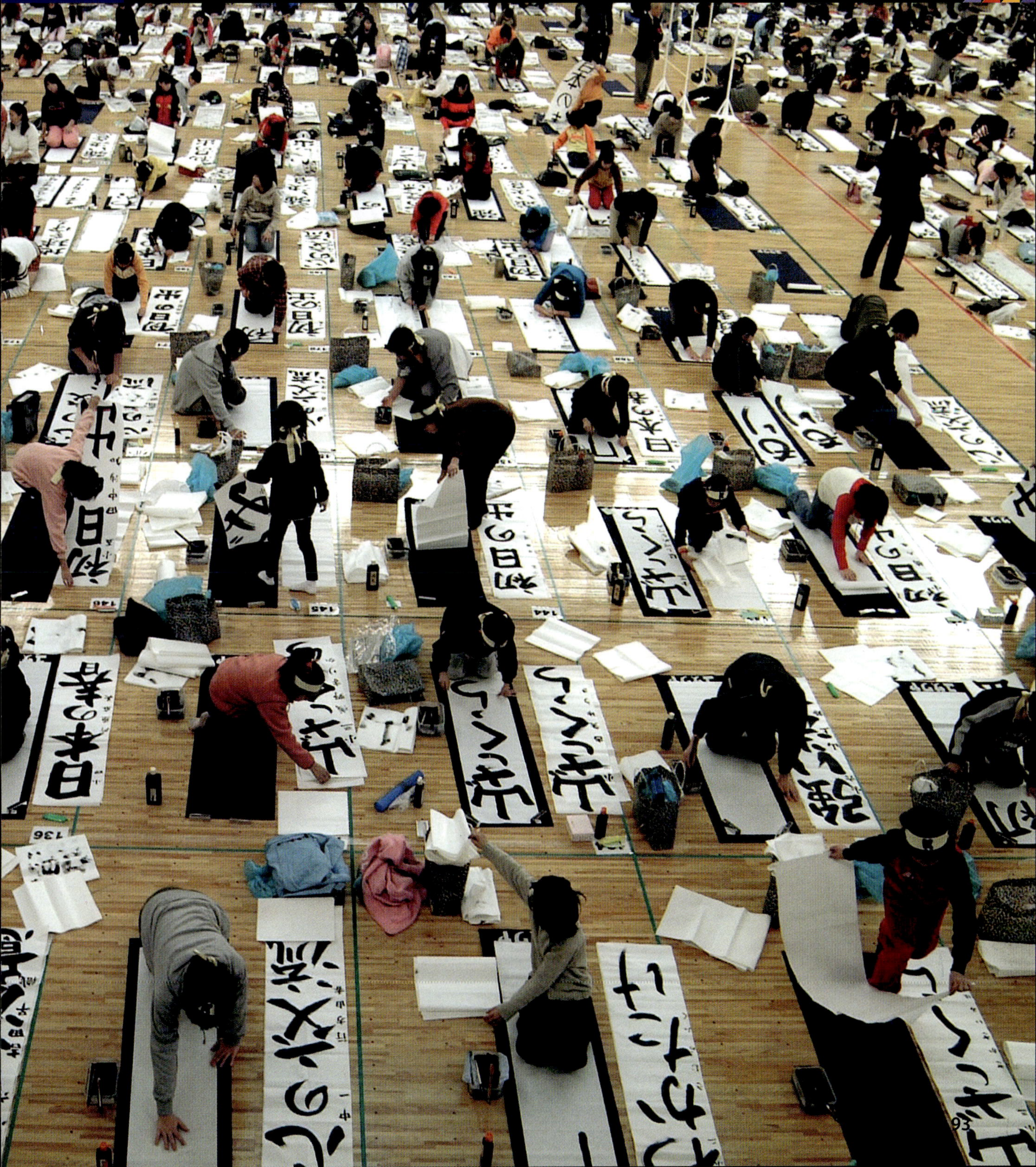

D Work with a partner. Read these quotations about writing and the creative process and discuss the questions.

1. What does each quotation mean?

2. Do you agree with the quotations? Check (✓) *Agree* or *Disagree*.

The Writer's Way

AGREE   DISAGREE

1. That which we persist in doing becomes easier, not that the task itself has become easier but that our ability to perform it has improved.
   –Ralph Waldo Emerson (1803–1882)

2. Here is a golden rule... Write legibly. The average temper of the human race would be perceptibly sweetened, if everybody obeyed this rule.
   –Lewis Carroll (1832–1898)

3. Energy and persistence alter all things.
   –Benjamin Franklin (1705–1790)

4. It's not the hours you put in your work that count, it's the work you put in the hours.
   –Sam Ewing (1949–)

E Work in a group and discuss your answers. Explain why you checked *Agree* or *Disagree*.

READING

READING 1 | Two Styles of Writing

You are going to read an article from an education journal on two different styles of writing English text. Use the article to gather information and ideas for your Unit Assignment.

PREVIEW THE READING

A. **PREVIEW** Think about how you write. What is important to you when you start to write something? Check (✓) all the characteristics that you pay attention to.

- ☐ My handwriting is legible.
- ☐ I write quickly.
- ☐ My handwriting is neat.
- ☐ My handwriting looks nice.
- ☐ My handwriting is different from everyone else's.
- ☐ I write using a certain type of pen or color of ink.

B. **QUICK WRITE** Think about learning to write the characters in your language and/or the letters in English. Were the characters difficult to learn? Did you ever tear the paper or have trouble making the writing look nice? How is your handwriting now? Write for 5–10 minutes in response. Be sure to use this section for your Unit Assignment.

C. **VOCABULARY** Check (✓) the words you know. Use a dictionary to define any new or unknown words. Then discuss how the words will relate to the unit with a partner.

advocate (v.)	legible (adj.)
alternative (n.) 🔑	maintain (v.) 🔑
attain (v.)	nerve (n.) 🔑
by hand (phr.)	proficient (adj.)
distinctive (adj.)	stimulate (v.)
ensure (v.) 🔑	worthwhile (adj.)

🔑 Oxford 3000™ words

D. Go online to listen and practice your pronunciation.

WORK WITH THE READING

Two Styles of Writing

a child learning to write

1   What does it mean to learn a language? Of course, we need to produce the sounds that make up words, put words together into meaningful units, and understand others who speak to us. To be literate, we also need to read and write. We should be able to write the letters of the alphabet, but with all the other parts of the language that need to be practiced, is it important to learn two ways to write them?

2   Educators have long seen the connection between learning to read and learning to write the letters that make up words. In one study, adults who learned to write a new alphabet with paper and pencil were better able to recognize and remember letters than their counterparts, who only studied the printed letters but did not try to form them. In addition, children develop fine motor skills and control when learning to write **by hand**. They must pay attention to the shape of the letters, for example, in order to produce a "d" that is distinct from a "b." Likewise, they must judge how much pressure to apply so as to avoid poking holes in the paper or accidentally tearing it. They must learn to move their hands and not smudge their work while writing. Also, they need to keep the words in a straight line and pay attention to how the letters are placed with respect to one another. For example, the stem of a "b" rises, while the stem of a "p" falls.

3   Educators also employ tactile[1] and kinesthetic[2] methods to help young children learn to form their letters. Children may trace letters on sandpaper to **stimulate** nerve endings in their fingers. Similarly, they may use their whole arm and shoulder to write giant letters in the sand or on big pieces of paper. Using these large muscle groups helps to establish important **nerve** connections between the muscles and the brain.

4   With so many subjects competing for attention, some parents and teachers have raised questions about how **worthwhile** it is to teach children both to print, to form letters in much the same way as they are seen in books, and to write in cursive, a kind of writing that connects the letters of a word together. Is it worth the time spent on learning both forms, or is it enough to learn just to print, leaving more time for other subjects, such as reading or computer skills?

---

[1] **tactile:** related to touch
[2] **kinesthetic:** related to motion

5   Supporters of learning both forms **maintain** that cursive writing is faster than printing—an advantage when composing papers or taking notes. Brian Palmer, writing in the online magazine *Slate*, states that cultures have favored connected script throughout time, and writers will often develop their own **distinctive** methods of linking letters so as to take advantage of the faster means of forming words. These individual scripts can be problematic for readers, however, so teachers **advocate** the use of a standard script so as to better **ensure** legibility.

6   Furthermore, because cursive writing is highly individualistic, it is used as a means to establish identity. Analysts can use handwritten documents to determine whether two samples of writing most likely came from the same person or not. This is useful to historians who find unsigned papers or to police looking at evidence.

7   Yet another reason for continuing to teach cursive writing is that it is part of our culture and, therefore, valuable to link us to our past. Indeed, cursive writing is often seen as a more mature type of writing, and if we want to continue to read historic documents that predate the printing press, we will almost certainly need to continue to teach children this form of writing.

8   Those who disagree with continuing to teach this form are not opposed to cursive writing in itself. They contend that not everyone needs to be **proficient** in this skill and that there are other solutions to the problems cursive writing addresses.

9   First of all, the neurological benefits of learning to write are developed both with printing and with cursive writing. As long as we continue to have children write with their hands, or do other skills with their hands that involve fine motor control, we will continue to build nerve connections. These benefits do not change.

Many people find typing a useful alternative.

10   In addition, even with instruction, children and adults do not always develop **legible** handwriting. Some people prefer to print and can actually **attain** writing speeds comparable to those of people writing in cursive. Many people find typing a useful **alternative** and have increased their speed so that they can take notes comfortably on a computer. Writers themselves have a responsibility to their readers to produce clear texts by printing or typing their words if their writing is illegible.

11   Options also exist for using handwriting as a means of identification. Instead of asking for a signature, a legal paper could carry a thumbprint or a fingerprint. Some people might choose to learn to read and write in cursive much like some people learn to make clothes, speak Latin, or build houses. These people could be called on to use their skills when an old document needs to be read or when a special document is created.

12   No one seems to be suggesting that we stop teaching children to write by hand. After all, even if we had the technology to replace writing, technology sometimes fails or is unavailable. As with any skill, handwriting needs to be practiced, and schools are under pressure to have time to practice many different skills. The question lies in whether we want to take the time and make the effort to teach children a second, related, form of writing. What do you think?

B. **VOCABULARY** Here are some words and phrases from Reading 1. Read
the sentences. Circle the answer that best matches the meaning of each
bold word or phrase.

1. My computer stopped working, so I wrote my essay **by hand.**
   a. using a machine
   b. easily
   c. with the hand(s)

2. When his heart stopped, the doctors **stimulated** it to keep him alive.
   a. made up
   b. made active
   c. made quiet

3. Your hands are sensitive because you have a lot of **nerves** in them.
   a. things that let you move or feel pain
   b. lines
   c. shaking

4. All our practice was **worthwhile** because we won the game.
   a. useless
   b. hard work over a long time
   c. good to spend time on or put effort into

5. Some people **maintain** that writing in cursive is still necessary.
   a. keep at the same level
   b. keep stating that something is true
   c. keep repaired

6. My teacher identified my **distinctive** handwriting when she looked at
   my note.
   a. different from others
   b. unpleasant in sound
   c. not loud enough to hear

7. He is going to **advocate** for a typing class next semester.
   a. publically support
   b. work hard at
   c. give legal advice to

8. Her mother **ensured** that she studied for the test.
   a. gave money when something happened
   b. made sure that something happened
   c. found out why something happened

9. It took hard work to become **proficient** in writing Chinese script.
   a. able to identify something
   b. able to support something
   c. able to do something well

10. A teacher's writing needs to be **legible** to students.
   a. legal; able to stand in court
   b. able to be selected
   c. clear enough to read

11. After four years, we will **attain** a university degree.
   a. put into
   b. succeed in getting
   c. understand

12. We didn't like our decision, but we didn't like the **alternative,** either.
   a. something that you change
   b. something that you charge
   c. something that you choose

iQ ONLINE   **C.** Go online for more practice with the vocabulary.

D. Circle the answer that best completes each statement.

1. Some benefits of writing by hand include ____.
   a. understanding differences in letters and gaining muscle control
   b. learning how to tear and poke holes in paper
   c. knowing different ways of writing

2. People disagree about whether ____.
   a. children should learn to write in school
   b. adults should learn to identify letters in another language
   c. children should learn to write in two different ways

3. Some benefits of writing in cursive are ____.
   a. it is faster and more legible than printing
   b. it is more attractive and stimulates more nerves
   c. it is faster and individualistic

4. People agree that ____.
   a. cursive writing is unnecessary
   b. children should learn to write by hand
   c. documents should be written by hand

E. Each subheading below refers to a main section of the text. Match the subheadings with the paragraph numbers in the box.

> paragraphs 2–3   paragraphs 5–7
>
> paragraph 4   paragraphs 8–11

1. Benefits of Writing by Hand: _________________________

2. Reasons for Teaching Cursive Writing: _________________________

3. Explanation of the Problem with Teaching Cursive Writing:

   ____

4. Reasons against Teaching Cursive Writing: _________________________

F. Write *T* (true) or *F* (false) for each statement. Then correct each false statement to make it true.

_____ 1. People who study letters in print and how to form them by hand learn the alphabet more quickly.

_____ 2. Tactile and kinesthetic methods of teaching can develop brain and nerve connections.

_____ 3. Brian Palmer states that most cultures through history have preferred printing over cursive writing.

_____ 4. Researchers can match a person's identity to a piece of handwriting.

_____ 5. Children must learn cursive in order to refine nerve connections and develop good motor skills.

G. Go online to read *Handmade Paper* and check your comprehension.

WRITE WHAT YOU THINK

A. Discuss these questions in a group.

1. Have you learned to write in two different ways? Why or why not?

2. Is it more important to learn to write by hand or to learn to use a computer keyboard? Why?

3. Do you think people will always write with pen and paper? Why or why not?

B. Choose one question and write a paragraph in response. Look back at your Quick Write on page 95 as you think about what you learned.

Writers **compare and contrast** information in order to examine the similarities and differences between two subjects. Comparisons show the subjects' similarities, while contrasts examine their differences. There are many different ways that texts can be organized when writers compare and contrast information. You can use a simple **T-chart** to quickly identify and separate the information about the two subjects. For example, look at the paragraph and the chart below.

There are a number of differences between printing and writing in cursive. The most obvious is that the <u>letters in print are separate</u> while the <u>letters in cursive writing are connected</u>. <u>Printed letters</u> also tend to be <u>more legible</u>, whereas <u>letters written in cursive</u> tend to be <u>less clear and harder to read</u>. Most children used to learn to write in both styles by the time they were ten years old.

Printing	Cursive
separate letters	connected letters
more legible	less clear; harder to read

You can also divide the information further by adding categories or topic areas down the side of the chart. (Look at the chart below.) After you chart the information, you can easily examine the ideas for similarities and differences.

A. Reread paragraphs 5–11 of Reading 1 on page 97. Underline the good and bad points about print and cursive. Then write the information in the chart below.

Critical Thinking (Tip)

In Activity A, you have to **categorize** information from Reading 1. When you categorize information, you can see more clearly how ideas are similar and different.

	Print	Cursive
Speed		
Legibility		
Choice		
Part of culture		

B. Discuss your chart with a partner and add any points that you missed. Do you see similarities and differences in the points?

C. Go online for more practice understanding compare and contrast organization.

READING 2 | Haji Noor Deen—A Chinese Muslim Calligrapher

You are going to read a brief biography of Haji Noor Deen, a famous artist who does calligraphy. Calligraphy is beautiful handwriting that people do with a special pen or brush. Use the biography to gather information and ideas for your Unit Assignment.

PREVIEW THE READING

A. **PREVIEW** You will learn about Haji Noor Deen's work as a calligrapher and how he feels about it. What do you expect to learn about his work as a calligrapher? Add three things to the list.

why he likes calligraphy

____

____

____

B. **QUICK WRITE** Would you want to learn calligraphy? Write for 5–10 minutes in response. Be sure to use this section for your Unit Assignment.

C. **VOCABULARY** Check (✓) the words you know. Then work with a partner to locate each word in the reading. Use clues to help define the words you don't know. Check your definitions in the dictionary.

complement *(n.)*	inspire *(v.)*
craft *(n.)* 🔑	recognize *(v.)* 🔑
determination *(n.)* 🔑	talent *(n.)* 🔑
essentially *(adv.)* 🔑	undertake *(v.)*
exhibit *(v.)* 🔑	unique *(adj.)* 🔑
imagery *(n.)*	

🔑 Oxford 3000™ words

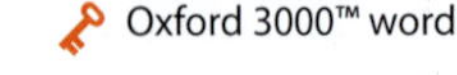

D. Go online to listen and practice your pronunciation.

WORK WITH THE READING

A. Read the biography and gather information about how important it is to write by hand.

HAJI NOOR DEEN—A CHINESE MUSLIM CALLIGRAPHER

1   Today, there are approximately twenty million Muslims in China, and Haji Noor Deen is one of them. Born in 1963 in Shangdong province, China, Haji Noor Deen Mi Guang Jiang is a well-known and respected calligrapher. What makes him **unique** is that he is a master of Arabic calligraphy. **Essentially**, his work is a calligraphic technique which combines both Chinese and Arabic scripts.

Haji Noor Deen

2   Of his work Deen has said, "As a Chinese Muslim calligrapher, I have a deep sense of responsibility in promoting, propagating, and carrying forward this intricate skill and precious cultural heritage." He has **undertaken** the task of not only producing his own style of calligraphy, but also of **inspiring** others through lectures and workshops. He has taught his **craft** in lectures and workshops at many prestigious institutions in the U.S. and the U.K., such as Harvard University, the University of Cambridge, the University of California, and Boston University.

3   In 1997, Haji Noor Deen was awarded the Certificate of Arabic Calligrapher in Egypt. He was the first Chinese person to be given this prestigious award. In 2000, Deen taught the first Arabic Calligraphy course at the Zhengzhou Islamic College in China. In 2008, he became the first Chinese student to study traditional Arabic calligraphy when he traveled to Istanbul and studied under two distinguished calligraphers, Shiek Hassan Jalabi and Dawoud Baktash. In an article in ArabNews.com, Afra Naushad names Deen as one of the "top influential Muslims of 2009."

4   Deen's work has been collected and displayed in museums around the world, where he is **recognized** for being the first Chinese/Arabic calligrapher. He has **exhibited** his work in many countries, including the U.S. (in a San Francisco museum and the Harvard University Museum), the U.K. (in the British Museum and the National Museum of Scotland), Ireland, Australia, Canada, and Singapore. In the Middle East, his work has been shown in the United Arab Emirates, Qatar, and Kuwait.

5   Naushad says, "Most of the pieces of his calligraphic work are a creative exaltation[1] celebrating the glory of God with the verses of the Holy Qur'an." Naushad describes Deen's calligraphy as a revival of Islamic creativity and the role it has played in the preservation of the Qur'an's message.

Haji Noor Deen's calligraphy

6   Deen's website states that some of the most beautiful names of Allah and the **imagery** of prostration[2] are presented using a combination of the Chinese and Arabic alphabets. In 2005, a piece of his calligraphy entitled *The 99 names of God* was acquired by the British Museum and is now permanently displayed there.

7   Deen's work reflects a dedication to the presentation of the unity of Arabic and Chinese cultures. Chinese and Arabic calligraphy are two of the world's most beautiful styles of writing. They are both opposites and **complements**. Deen's calligraphy demonstrates that when combined, the result is a writing style of unique beauty.

8   "With **determination** and perseverance, with my hands and with the knowledge and **talent** bestowed on me by Allah the Almighty, I will seek to continue to craft the majestic and aesthetically[3] pleasing cultural tradition," Deen said.

---

[1] **exaltation:** a feeling of very great joy or happiness
[2] **prostration:** the act of stretching out with one's face on the ground, often in prayer
[3] **aesthetically:** beautifully; in a pleasing manner

B. **VOCABULARY** Here are some words from Reading 2. Read the sentences. Then write each bold word next to the correct definition. You may need to change verbs to their base form and nouns to the singular form.

1. It takes many years of practice to perfect the **craft** of calligraphy.

2. The children's stories were **exhibited** in the classroom.

3. They work well together because their methods of working are **essentially** the same.

4. A good teacher should be capable of **inspiring** his or her students to do well.

5. I believe he has the **determination** to achieve his goals.

6. These two foods are often eaten together because they are **complements**.

7. They were **recognized** for their acts of kindness to others.

8. The **imagery** in the story helped the young readers understand and feel sympathy for the characters.

9. Joshua has always had a **talent** for math. At a young age, he could see patterns and relationships between numbers and was able to understand complex equations.

10. I have never seen another book like that one. It is **unique**.

11. William is going to **undertake** the task of organizing the stories the students wrote into a book.

a. ___________________ (*n.*) an activity involving a special skill at making things with your hands

b. ___________________ (*adv.*) basically; when you consider the most important part of something

c. ___________________ (*v.*) to give someone the desire or enthusiasm to do well

d. ___________________ (*n.*) a natural skill or ability

e. ___________________ (*v.*) to agree that you will do something; to carry out

f. ___________________ (*v.*) to show something to the public

g. _________________ (*n.*) the use of descriptions and comparisons in language in order to have a strong effect on people's imagination and emotions

h. _________________ (*n.*) a thing that goes together well with something else

i. _________________ (*adj.*) unlike anything else; being the only one of its type

j. _________________ (*n.*) the continuation of something even though it is difficult or people say you cannot do it

k. _________________ (*v.*) to show that you think something that someone has done is good

iQ ONLINE   **C.** Go online for more practice with the vocabulary.

D. Write *T* (true) or *F* (false) for each statement. Then correct each false statement to make it true. Write the paragraph number where you found information to support your answer.

Haji Noor Deen . . .

_____ 1. learned calligraphy at Harvard University. (paragraph _____)

____

_____ 2. has exhibited his calligraphy in museums. (paragraph _____)

____

_____ 3. teaches and gives workshops. (paragraph _____)

____

_____ 4. is well known in the world. (paragraph _____)

____

_____ 5. considers calligraphy an important cultural heritage. (paragraph _____)

____

_____ 6. has just retired from calligraphy. (paragraph _____)

____

_____ 7. was born in China. (paragraph _____)

____

E. **Number the events in the order in which they occurred.**

____ **1.** Haji Noor Deen was awarded the Certificate of Arabic Calligrapher in Egypt.

____ **2.** The British Museum acquired a piece of Deen's calligraphy.

____ **3.** Deen became the first Chinese student to study traditional Arabic calligraphy.

____ **4.** Deen taught the first Arabic Calligraphy course at the Zhengzhou Islamic College.

____ **5.** Deen was listed in the "top influential Muslims."

F. **Answer these questions to add information to each event in Haji Noor Deen's life from Activity E.**

1. What is noteworthy about his being awarded the Certificate of Arabic Calligrapher in Egypt?

____

2. What is the name of the piece of calligraphy in the British Museum?

____

3. Where did he study traditional Arabic calligraphy?

____

4. Outside of China, where has Haji Noor Deen taught calligraphy?

____

5. Where and by whom was he listed in the "top influential Muslims"?

____

G. **List the reasons why Haji Noor Deen combines the styles of Arabic and Chinese calligraphy in his work.**

____

____

____

WRITE WHAT YOU THINK

A. Discuss the questions in a group. Look back at your Quick Write on page 102 as you think about what you learned.

1. Why does Haji Noor Deen feel he has a responsibility to promote calligraphy?

2. Is it possible for anyone to learn calligraphy?

B. Before you watch the video, discuss the questions in a group.

1. What are three reasons for continuing to teach cursive writing in school?

2. Is cursive writing as important a skill as calligraphy?

3. Is learning cursive a good use of time in school? Are there other subjects that are more important?

C. Go online to watch the video about the importance of handwriting. Then check your comprehension.

VIDEO VOCABULARY

bill *(n.)* a plan for a possible new law

cognition *(n.)* conscious mental activity

heritage *(n.)* the history, traditions, and qualities that a country or society has had for many years and that are considered an important part of its character

infusion *(n.)* the addition of something that is needed or helpful

nostalgia *(n.)* a feeling of affection, mixed with sadness, for things that are in the past

D. Think about the unit video, Reading 1, and Reading 2 as you discuss the questions. Then choose one question and write a paragraph in response.

1. What are some similarities between English writing and Arabic calligraphy?

2. What are some differences between English writing and Arabic calligraphy?

Finding the correct meaning

There are many words that have the same spelling and pronunciation but different meanings. These words are called **homonyms**.

> *bank* **(n.)** *an organization that provides various financial services*
>
> My salary is paid directly into my **bank**.
>
> *bank* **(n.)** *the side of a river and the land near it*
>
> She jumped into the river and swam to the opposite **bank**.

Some homonyms may be different parts of speech, for example, a noun with one or more meanings and a verb with other meanings.

> *place* **(n.)** *a particular position, point, or area*
>
> This would be a good **place** for a picnic.
>
> *place* **(v.)** *to put something in a particular place, especially when you*
> *do it carefully*
>
> He carefully **placed** his hand on his son's shoulder.

Advanced dictionaries will list all the word forms and definitions for them. When using a dictionary to find the correct meaning of a word, it is important to read the entire sentence and consider the use and context.

All dictionary entries are from the *Oxford Advanced American Dictionary for learners of English* © Oxford University Press 2011.

A. Look at the dictionary entry for *craft*. Check (✓) the correct information.

1. *Craft* can be used as:
- ☐ an adjective
- ☐ an adverb
- ☐ a noun
- ☐ a verb

2. *Craft* can mean:
- ☐ a boat
- ☐ a skill
- ☐ frightening
- ☐ strange
- ☐ to make
- ☐ to give

craft /kræft/ *noun, verb*

● *noun* **1** [C, U] an activity involving a special skill at making things with your hands: *traditional crafts like basket-weaving* ◆ *a craft fair/workshop* ⊃ see also ARTS AND CRAFTS **2** [sing.] all the skills needed for a particular activity: *chefs who learned their craft in five-star hotels* ◆ *the writer's craft* **3** [U] (*formal*, *disapproving*) skill in making people believe what you want them to believe: *He knew how to win by craft and diplomacy what he could not gain by force.* **4** [C] (*pl.* **craft**) a boat or ship: *Hundreds of small craft bobbed around the liner as it steamed into the harbor.* ◆ *a landing/pleasure craft* **5** [C] (*pl.* **craft**) an aircraft or SPACECRAFT

● *verb* [usually passive] **~ sth** to make something using special skills, especially with your hands **SYN** FASHION: *All the furniture is crafted from natural materials.* ◆ *a carefully crafted speech* ⊃ see also HANDCRAFTED

B. Read the sentences and phrases from Readings 1 and 2. Look up each bold word in your dictionary. Write the part of speech and the correct definition based on the context.

Reading 1 (pages 96–97)

1. Children may trace letters on sandpaper to **stimulate** nerve endings in their fingers. (paragraph 3)

   ____

2. Using these large muscle groups helps to establish important **nerve** connections between the muscles and the brain. (paragraph 3)

   ____

3. Supporters of learning both forms **maintain** that cursive writing is faster than printing. (paragraph 5)

   ____

4. Some people prefer to print and can actually **attain** writing speeds comparable to those of people writing in cursive. (paragraph 10)

   ____

Reading 2 (pages 103–104)

5. What makes him **unique** is that he is a master of Arabic calligraphy. (paragraph 1)

   ____

6. He has **undertaken** the task of not only producing his own style of calligraphy . . . (paragraph 2)

   ____

7. . . . but also of **inspiring** others through lectures and workshops. (paragraph 2)

   ____

8. . . . some of the most beautiful names of Allah and the **imagery** of prostration . . . (paragraph 6)

   ____

C. Go online for more practice with using the dictionary to distinguish between homonyms.

WRITING

At the end of this unit, you will write an essay comparing and contrasting two forms of writing. This essay will include specific information from the readings, the unit video, and your own ideas.

Writing Skill | Writing a compare and contrast essay

A **compare and contrast essay** describes the similarities and differences between two subjects. Comparisons show their similarities, while contrasts examine their differences.

Introduction

The introduction describes the two subjects being compared and contrasted. It has a thesis statement that explains the relationship between the two subjects or gives reasons why the relationship is important.

Body paragraphs

There are many different ways to organize the body paragraphs of a compare and contrast essay. Before you write a compare and contrast essay, it is important to decide which organization is best for your essay. Here are two ways to organize your ideas:

- In a **point by point essay,** you choose three or more key points to compare and contrast. Each body paragraph compares and contrasts one key point. This organization can be best when you want to balance your essay evenly between your two subjects.
- In a **similarities and differences essay,** the first body paragraph explains what is similar about the two subjects. The second body paragraph explains what is different about the two subjects. The third body paragraph discusses the most important similarities and differences. This organization can be best when you want to explain why one subject is better than the other subject.

Conclusion

The conclusion summarizes the similarities and differences and gives the writer's opinion about the topic. It can explain why one of the subjects is better than the other or why they are of equal value.

Writing in the Digital Age

As we move more firmly into the digital age, we are writing as much or more with keyboards as with pen and paper. Computers and smartphones are basic equipment in the business community, and students are more likely to have to type their papers than to write by hand. While both methods serve the purpose of putting words into visible text, there are also some important differences.

Both handwriting and typing are used to convey information. They both use the same groups of letters to form words and the same groups of words to form sentences. However, in handwritten text, all of the beauty and the flaws are attributed to the writer, and more information about the author, especially emotion, can come out. The appearance of handwritten text can change easily with fatigue or excitement, while typewritten words look the same regardless of whether they were produced by a tired author or by a delighted one. Because type is standardized, there are no flourishes or misshapen letters to worry about.

Speed is a second factor in writing. Writers like to be able to get their ideas down, in ink or electrons, as they come, moving them from the brain, through the hand, to the paper or screen. Taking notes in a meeting or a class, which requires the writer to process someone else's ideas, is facilitated by having fluency in writing or typing. Using a pen and paper requires an author to keep an eye on the words so that they are legible—in a line, not overlapping, not too big or too small. Learning to "touch-type," on the other hand, frees the writer from looking at the words, so more attention can be paid to the actual ideas.

Both types of writing convey information to a reader, whether the reader is a stranger, a close friend, or the writer himself. Misspellings, awkward sentences, and incorrect grammar can be found in both handwritten and typed text. It is much easier to get away with an error in handwriting than in print. In handwritten text, a character can be ambiguous—is that an *a* or an *o*?—whereas a choice must be made when a keyboard is used. Although a person writing by hand must usually rely on himself for spacing within and between words, for respecting margins, and for correcting errors, most word processing programs take care of such spacing and layout concerns automatically, and some will correct common misspellings and other errors.

In short, words convey ideas, whether they are handwritten or typed. They use the same symbols, with some minor variations, and can be produced at varying speeds. The more personalized handwriting lends itself to showing individualization, paying attention to the skill, and error, while the mechanized writing demonstrates regularity, automatic responses, and a nudge toward corrections. Which is better? That might be in the hands of the writer—or in the eyes of the reader. Either way, we will no doubt have both forms with us for years to come.

1. What is the thesis statement? Underline it.

2. How is the essay organized? ____

3. Why do you think the author organized it this way?

____

B. Reread the essay on page 112. Complete the chart with both the similarities and the differences for each key point. Then compare with a partner.

Compare and Contrast Essay: Point by Point		
Key points	**Handwriting**	**Typing**
1. individualization	beauty and flaws are writers'	same characters; no variety in shape
2. attention to forms		
3. corrections		

C. Work with a partner. Complete the chart below. Reorganize the information in the essay into a plan for a similarities and differences essay. Use the chart in Activity B to help you.

Compare and Contrast Essay: Similarities and Differences		
Similarities	**Differences**	
	Handwriting	**Typing**
convey information	beauty and flaws are writers'	same characters; no variety in shape

D. You can use the same type of chart to help you brainstorm your ideas. Use the chart below to help you think of examples of what you could write about cooking 100 years ago and cooking now.

Compare and Contrast Essay: Similarities and Differences in Cooking 100 Years Ago and Now		
Similarities	Differences	
	100 years ago	Now

E. Choose another craft or activity you are familiar with. Create a chart for that activity like the one in Activity D.

Compare and Contrast Essay: Similarities and Differences in ______________		
Similarities	Differences	
	100 years ago	Now

Do-It-Yourself, Then and Now

Tap, tap, tap. "Ouch!" I had hit my thumb one more time with the hammer, so I decided to take a break from building a new bookcase. I realized that I was actually enjoying working on this project, despite the pain in my thumb, because I liked doing something practical and having something new at the end of the day. I had become part of a trend of crafters making things by hand, not because they have to but because they want to. In the past few years, do-it-yourself (DIY) projects have become increasingly popular, but they are different from how they used to be.

In the past, getting food, clothing, and shelter often required having the skills to raise animals and plants for food, to make clothes, and to build and repair houses and other structures. There were no prepackaged foods, so girls, mostly, learned to cook. Because ready-made clothes were expensive, girls were taught how to make their own. Both girls and boys tended gardens and animals to supplement their families' diets. Boys often learned to construct and repair simple furniture and buildings by learning elementary carpentry, masonry, and plumbing. These skills were necessary to remain fed, clothed, and protected from the elements.

Nowadays, on the other hand, people can choose which, if any, of these skills they want to learn. With more available off-the-shelf products and more disposable income, more people buy food and clothing rather than making them themselves. They can move into existing housing and hire someone to do the necessary repairs. Despite all this, there has been a rise in the number of people learning these skills. Some cite the enjoyment of doing something practical with their hands, while others mention the satisfaction of creating, or helping to create, food, clothing, structures, or other materials by themselves. Furthermore, these skills are not typically divided by gender: Men may cook new types of food, and women may find themselves with a hammer and a blueprint.

Learning practical skills, like sewing and woodworking, may not be for everyone, but many people are finding that they enjoy the process of creating their own items, whether a new sweater, an additional closet, or a meal from their own garden. Without the necessity of making many things ourselves, we can enjoy the art and satisfaction of doing things ourselves. Why don't you give it a try?

1. What is the thesis statement? Underline it.

2. How is the essay organized? _______________________________

   Why do you think the author organized it this way? _______________

   ____

G. Go online for more practice with writing a compare and contrast essay.

Grammar **Subordinators and transitions to compare and contrast**

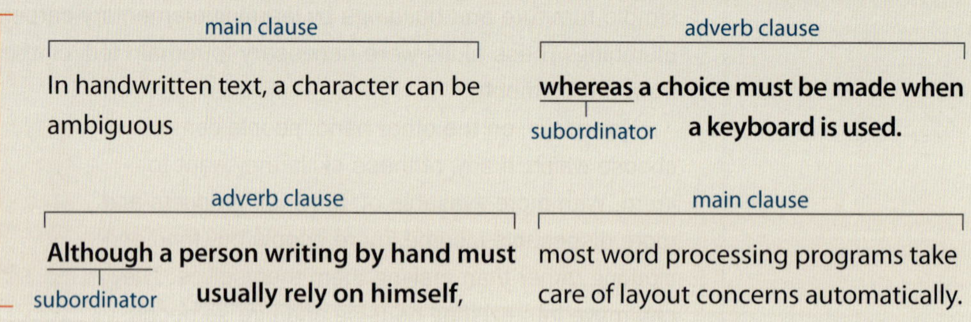

You can use a number of different words and phrases to compare and contrast ideas.

Subordinators showing contrast

You can use some adverb clauses to show an idea that contrasts with the main clause. The subordinators *although* and *though* show contrasting ideas. *Whereas* and *while* often show more direct opposition. Notice the comma when the adverb clause comes first.

main clause	adverb clause
In handwritten text, a character can be ambiguous	**whereas** a choice must be made when a keyboard is used.
	subordinator

adverb clause	main clause
Although a person writing by hand must usually rely on himself,	most word processing programs take care of layout concerns automatically.
subordinator	

Transitions showing comparison

You can use some transition words to show comparison. Some common transition words to show comparison are *similarly*, *likewise*, and *in addition*. These are used to discuss similarities.

> Children may trace letters on sandpaper. **Similarly**, they may use their whole arm and shoulder to write giant letters.
>
> They must pay attention to the shape of the letters. **Likewise**, they must judge how much pressure to apply.

Transitions showing contrast

You can use some transition words to show contrast, or differences.

Contrast	More direct opposition	Concession	
however	on the other hand	nevertheless	in spite of this
though	in contrast	nonetheless	despite this

Both handwriting and typing use the same groups of letters to form words. **However**, in handwritten text, all of the beauty and the flaws are attributed to the writer.

Using a pen and paper requires an author to keep an eye on the words. Learning to "touch-type," **on the other hand**, frees the writer from looking at the words.

A. **Read each sentence. Underline the word or phrase that indicates a comparison or a contrast. Then write CP (comparison) or CT (contrast).**

____ 1.   Although some calligraphers use this craft as their job, others use it just for enjoyment.

____ 2.   Writing well takes practice. Similarly, doing well at any activity takes commitment and training.

____ 3.   There are professionals in many activities. Nonetheless, amateurs can also benefit from trying their hands at different hobbies.

____ 4.   Whereas some hobbies require a lot of time to learn, others can be learned easily.

____ 5.   Hobbies can help us relax. Likewise, they can help us enjoy time with others.

B. **Circle the best phrase to complete each sentence.**

1. John likes to use his hands to make things while Robert (prefers to play sports / makes things by hand, too).

2. John put together his own computer. Similarly, his brother (would rather go fishing / built a computer, too).

3. Robert likes to go fishing and camping. Though he enjoys both, he (likes camping better / likes them both equally).

4. Robert hopes to spend his weekend on the beach. John, too, plans to (study in the library / go to the beach).

5. Robert and John spend a lot of time studying. Nonetheless, they find they (need to study / appreciate having time to relax).

6. Although Robert wants to sleep in a tent, John will (sleep outside / sleep in a tent, too).

C. Complete these sentences using your own ideas. Make sure you use correct punctuation.

1. I don't enjoy fishing very much. Nevertheless *, I enjoy cooking and eating the fish.*

2. Although many people enjoy fishing ________________________

3. Not many people become professional athletes. Likewise ________________________

4. Professional soccer players often have rigorous training. On the other hand ________________________

5. I like both soccer and handball. However ________________________

6. Whereas some athletes end their careers early ________________________

7. Athletes need ambition to succeed. Similarly ________________________

D. Go online for more practice with subordinators and transitions to compare and contrast.

E. Go online for the grammar expansion.

In this assignment, you are going to write a five-paragraph essay to compare and contrast two methods of writing. As you prepare your essay, think about the Unit Question, "How important is it to write by hand?" Use information from Reading 1, Reading 2, the unit video, and your work in this unit to support your essay. Refer to the Self-Assessment checklist on page 120.

Go to the Online Writing Tutor for a writing model and alternate Unit Assignments.

PLAN AND WRITE

When you brainstorm ideas using both a point by point chart and a similarities and differences chart, it will help you discover which organization works best for your subject, and you may get more ideas.

A. BRAINSTORM Follow these steps to help you organize your ideas.

1. Work with a partner. Discuss pairs of methods of writing, such as writing in Chinese and writing in English or printed Arabic and handwritten Arabic, that you think have an interesting or important relationship to each other.

2. Choose the two methods of writing you would like to use as your subject to compare and contrast.

3. Write points to compare and contrast and similarities and differences for your subject. (Refer to the charts on page 113 to help you organize your ideas.)

B. PLAN Follow these steps to plan your essay.

1. Look at your ideas from question 3 in Activity A. Decide whether your essay would be best organized as a point by point essay or a similarities and differences essay.

2. Go to the Online Resources to download and complete the graphic organizer for your compare and contrast essay (point by point or similarities and differences).

3. Go to the Online Resources to download and complete the outline for your compare and contrast essay.

C. WRITE Use your PLAN notes to write your essay. Go to *iQ Online* to use the Online Writing Tutor.

1. Write your essay comparing and contrasting two methods of writing. Be sure to include an introduction with a thesis statement, three body paragraphs, and a conclusion.

2. Look at the Self-Assessment checklist on page 120 to guide your writing.

REVISE AND EDIT

A. **PEER REVIEW** Read your partner's essay. Then go online and use the Peer Review worksheet. Discuss the review with your partner.

B. **REWRITE** Based on your partner's review, revise, and rewrite your essay.

C. **WRITE** Complete the Self-Assessment checklist as you prepare to write the final draft of your essay. Be prepared to hand in your work or discuss it in class.

SELF-ASSESSMENT		
Yes	No	
☐	☐	Does the thesis statement explain the relationship between the two subjects or give reasons why the relationship is important?
☐	☐	Is the essay organized using one of the compare and contrast essay types?
☐	☐	Does the essay contain an introduction, three body paragraphs, and a conclusion?
☐	☐	Does the essay use subordinators and transitions to compare and contrast?
☐	☐	Does the essay include vocabulary from the unit?
☐	☐	Did you check the essay for punctuation, spelling, and grammar?

D. **REFLECT** Go to the Online Discussion Board to discuss these questions.

1. What is something new you learned in this unit?

2. Look back at the Unit Question—How important is it to write by hand? Is your answer different now than when you started the unit? If yes, how is it different? Why?

TRACK YOUR SUCCESS

Circle the words and phrases you have learned in this unit.

Nouns
alternative 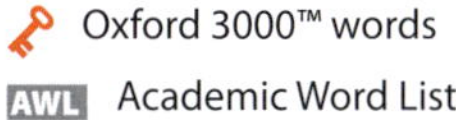 AWL
complement AWL
craft
determination
imagery AWL
nerve
talent

Verbs
advocate AWL
attain AWL
ensure AWL
exhibit AWL
inspire
maintain AWL
recognize
stimulate
undertake AWL

Adjectives
distinctive AWL
legible
proficient
unique AWL
worthwhile

Adverb
essentially

Phrase
by hand

Oxford 3000™ words
AWL Academic Word List

Check (✓) the skills you learned. If you need more work on a skill, refer to the page(s) in parentheses.

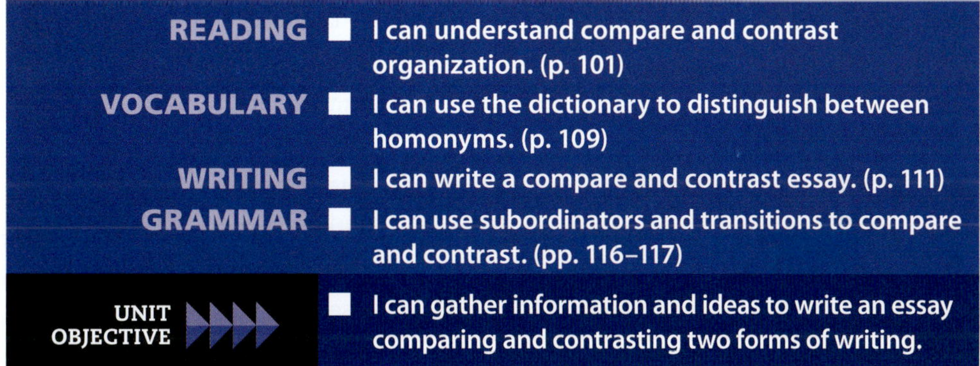

🔑 The keywords of the **Oxford 3000**™ have been carefully selected by a group of language experts and experienced teachers as the words which should receive priority in vocabulary study because of their importance and usefulness.

AWL The **Academic Word List** is the most principled and widely accepted list of academic words. Averil Coxhead gathered information from academic materials across the academic disciplines to create this word list.

The Common European Framework of Reference for Languages (CEFR) provides a basic description of what language learners have to do to use language effectively. The system contains 6 reference levels: **A1, A2, B1, B2, C1, C2**. CEFR leveling provided by the Word Family Framework, created by Richard West and published by the British Council. http://www.learnenglish.org.uk/wff/

UNIT 1

achievement (n.) 🔑 **AWL**, B1

acknowledged (for) (adj.) 🔑 **AWL**, C1

confront (v.) 🔑, B1

constrained (adj.) **AWL**, C1

criteria (n.) 🔑 **AWL**, A2

inclined (adj.) **AWL**, C1

inherently (adv.) **AWL**, C2

initiative (n.) 🔑 **AWL**, B2

pursue (v.) 🔑 **AWL**, A2

resolve (n.) 🔑 **AWL**, B2

version (n.) 🔑 **AWL**, B2

UNIT 2

concept (n.) 🔑 **AWL**, B2

distinguish (v.) 🔑, B2

evolve (v.) **AWL**, B1

feature (v.) 🔑 **AWL**, B2

focus on (phr. v.) 🔑 **AWL**, B2

in theory (idm.) 🔑 **AWL**, B2

individual (n.) 🔑 **AWL**, B1

investment (n.) 🔑 **AWL**, B2

liberate (v.) **AWL**, C1

mentally (adv.) 🔑 **AWL**, B2

minimize (v.) **AWL**, C1

negative (n.) 🔑 **AWL**, B2

neutral (adj.) **AWL**, B2

potential (adj.) 🔑 **AWL**, B2

priority (n.) 🔑 **AWL**, B2

promote (v.) 🔑 **AWL**, B2

remove (v.) 🔑 **AWL**, B2

residence (n.) **AWL**, B2

tend (v.) 🔑, B2

urban (adj.) 🔑, B2

visualize (v.) **AWL**, C2

UNIT 3

accurately (adv.) 🔑 **AWL**, B1

assumption (n.) **AWL**, B1

capture (v.) 🔑, B1

colleague (n.) 🔑 **AWL**, A2

consistent with (phr.) 🔑 **AWL**, B1

creative (adj.) 🔑 **AWL**, B1

equipped with (phr.) **AWL**, B2

exaggerate (v.) 🔑, C1

motivate (v.) **AWL**, B2

period (n.) 🔑 **AWL**, B1

rely on (phr. v.) 🔑 **AWL**, B2

select (v.) 🔑 **AWL**, B1

significance (n.) **AWL**, C1

suspect (v.) 🔑, B2

theoretically (adv.) **AWL**, C2

UNIT 4

advocate (v.) **AWL**, B2

alternative (n.) 🔑 **AWL**, B2

attain (v.) **AWL**, C1

complement (n.) **AWL**, C2

craft (n.) 🔑, B1

determination (n.) 🔑, B2

distinctive (adj.) **AWL**, B2

ensure (v.) 🔑 **AWL**, B2

essentially (adv.) 🔑, B2

exhibit (v.) 🔑 **AWL**, B2

imagery (n.) **AWL**, C2

maintain (v.) 🔑 **AWL**, B2

nerve (n.) 🔑, B1

recognize (v.) 🔑, B2

talent (n.) 🔑, B1

undertake (v.) **AWL**, B1

unique (adj.) 🔑 **AWL**, B2

UNIT 5

access (n.) 🔑 **AWL**, B1

approach (n.) 🔑 **AWL**, B2

benefit (n.) 🔑 **AWL**, B1

challenge (v.) 🔑 **AWL**, B2

contribute (v.) 🔑 **AWL**, B2

currently (adv.) 🔑, B2

eliminate (v.) 🔑 **AWL**, B1

encourage (v.) 🔑, B1

expert (n.) 🔑 **AWL**, B1

link (n.) 🔑 **AWL**, B2

major (adj.) 🔑 **AWL**, B2

modify (v.) **AWL**, C1

participate (v.) 🔑 **AWL**, B2

physical (adj.) 🔑 **AWL**, B2

practical (adj.) 🔑, B2

primarily (adv.) 🔑 **AWL**, B2

shift (v.) 🔑 **AWL**, B2

source (n.) 🔑 **AWL**, B2

stable (adj.) 🔑 **AWL**, B1

UNIT 6

acquire (v.) 🔑 **AWL**, B2

adjust (v.) 🔑 **AWL**, B2

ambiguous (adj.) **AWL**, C2

analyze (v.) 🔑 **AWL**, B2

anticipate (v.) 🔑 **AWL**, C1

approach (v.) 🔑 **AWL**, B1

constant (adj.) 🔑 **AWL**, B2

contact (v.) 🔑 **AWL**, A2

enable *(v.)* 🔑 AWL, B2
encounter *(v.)* 🔑 AWL, B2
expertise *(n.)* AWL, B2
fixed *(adj.)* 🔑, B2
incentive *(n.)* AWL, C2
income *(n.)* 🔑 AWL, B2
institution *(n.)* 🔑 AWL, B2
interpret *(v.)* 🔑 AWL, B2
particular *(adj.)* 🔑, B2
pattern *(n.)* 🔑, B2
permanent *(adj.)* 🔑, B1
reluctant *(adj.)* AWL, C1
transition *(n.)* 🔑 AWL, C1
utilize *(v.)* AWL, B2

UNIT 7

adopt *(v.)* 🔑, B2
cite *(v.)* AWL, B2
confirm *(v.)* 🔑 AWL, B2
conflict *(n.)* 🔑 AWL, B2
controversial *(adj.)* AWL, B2
extensive *(adj.)* 🔑, B2
genuinely *(adv.)* 🔑, B2
inevitable *(adj.)* 🔑 AWL, C1
intervene *(v.)* AWL, C2
moral *(adj.)* 🔑, B2
motive *(n.)* AWL, B2
preliminary *(adj.)* AWL, C1
significant *(adj.)* 🔑 AWL, B2
sustainable *(adj.)* AWL, C1

UNIT 8

beneficial *(adj.)* AWL, B2
complex *(adj.)* 🔑 AWL, B2
conduct *(v.)* 🔑 AWL, B2
conflicted *(adj.)* AWL, C1
consequently *(adv.)* AWL, B2
evident *(adj.)* AWL, B2
incorporate *(v.)* AWL, C2
inhibit *(v.)* AWL, C1
innovative *(adj.)* AWL, C1
regulate *(v.)* AWL, B2
rigid *(adj.)* AWL, B2
structured *(adj.)* 🔑 AWL, B2
vital *(adj.)* 🔑, B2

OXFORD
UNIVERSITY PRESS

198 Madison Avenue
New York, NY 10016 USA

Great Clarendon Street, Oxford, OX2 6DP, United Kingdom

Oxford University Press is a department of the University of Oxford.
It furthers the University's objective of excellence in research, scholarship,
and education by publishing worldwide. Oxford is a registered trade
mark of Oxford University Press in the UK and in certain other countries

Adult Content Director: Stephanie Karras
Publisher: Sharon Sargent
Managing Editor: Mariel DeKranis
Development Editor: Eric Zuarino
Head of Digital, Design, and Production: Bridget O'Lavin
Executive Art and Design Manager: Maj-Britt Hagsted
Design Project Manager: Debbie Lofaso
Content Production Manager: Julie Armstrong
Image Manager: Trisha Masterson
Image Editor: Liaht Ziskind
Production Coordinator: Brad Tucker

ISBN: 978 0 19 482071 4 Student Book 4A with iQ Online pack
ISBN: 978 0 19 482072 1 Student Book 4A as pack component
ISBN: 978 0 19 481802 5 iQ Online student website

Printed in China
This book is printed on paper from certified and well-managed sources.

ACKNOWLEDGEMENTS

*The authors and publisher are grateful to those who have given permission to
reproduce the following extracts and adaptations of copyright material:*
p. 13 Adaptation of "Search for 100 Real-Life Heroes" by Kate Hodal and
Tom Phillips, from *The Guardian*, December 23, 2011, http://www.
theguardian.com/world/2011/dec/23/100-real-heroes-search-tithiya-sharma.
Copyright Guardian News and Media Ltd 2011. Used by permission;
p. 36 From "So Much Dead Space" by Paco Underhill, *Conference Board Review*,
September/October 2006, Vol. 44, Issue 5. Used by permission of Paco
Underhill, www.pacounderhill.com; p. 73 Excerpt(s) from *Bird by Bird: Some
Instructions on Writing and Life* by Anne Lamott, copyright © 1994 by Anne
Lamott. Used by permission of Pantheon Books, an imprint of the Knopf
Doubleday Publishing Group, a division of Random House, LLC, and by
The Wylie Agency LLC. All rights reserved; p. 134 Reprinted from "Anatomy
of a Nutrition Trend," *Food Insight*, March/April 2002. Copyright © 2002
International Food Information Council Foundation. Used by permission
from the International Food Information Council Foundation;
p. 163 From "Making My First Post-College Decision," by Devin Reams, *Ready
or Not, Here Comes Life*, http://www.employeeevolution.com. Used by
permission of Devin Reams; p. 186 From "A tribe is discovered in a clearing
of the Brazilian rainforest: should we leave them alone or prepare them for
the 21st century" by Jeremy Watson, from *The Scotsman*, June 1, 2008,
Sunday edition, News.Scotsman.com. Copyright © The Scotsman
Publications Ltd. Used by permission; p. 194 "Is Alaska's Pebble Mine the
Next Keystone XL?" by Svati Kirsten Narula, from *The Atlantic*. Copyright
2014 The Atlantic Media Co. as published in *The Atlantic Magazine*, March 14,
2014. All rights reserved. Distributed by Tribune Content Agency, LLC.
Reprinted by permission; p. 214 "The Promise of Play" from *Play* by Stuart
Brown, with Christopher Vaughan, copyright © 2009 by Stuart Brown. Used
by permission of Avery Publishing, an imprint of Penguin Group (USA) LLC.

Illustrations by: p. 34 Stuart Bradford; p. 64 Stacy Merlin; p. 73 Barb Bastian;
p. 94 Stuart Bradford; p. 124 Stacy Merlin; p. 154 Stacy Merlin; p. 184 Stacy
Merlin; p. 194 5W Infographics; p. 212 Stacy Merlin.

*We would also like to thank the following for permission to reproduce the following
photographs:* Cover: Yongyut Kumsri/Shutterstock; Video Vocabulary (used
throughout the book): Oleksiy Mark/Shutterstock; p. 2 HO/Reuters/Corbis;
p. 3 William Whitehurst/Corbis, Adrian Sherratt/Alamy; p. 7 Blend Images/
Alamy (woodworking), Tetra Images/Alamy (injured child); p. 13 Duravitski/
Alamy; p. 14 Sonja Kruse The Ubuntu Girl; p. 33 Bizroug/Shutterstock;
p. 35 Satish Kaushik/The India Today Group/Getty Images; p. 36 imagebroker/
Alamy; p. 43 Stagedhomes.com/Staged Homes (all); p. 51 imageBROKER/
Superstock Ltd.; p. 53 Koksharov Dmitry/Shutterstock; p. 58 Image Source/
Alamy; p. 63 KidStock/Getty Images; p. 66 BananaStock/Thinkstock;
p. 72 Robert Manella/Getty Images; p. 83 beasty/Shutterstock; p. 88 Chris
Pancewicz/Alamy; p. 93 Kurita KAKU/Gamma-Rapho via Getty Images;
p. 96 allOver images/Alamy; p. 97 Ermolaev Alexander/Shutterstock;
pp. 103, 104 Marco Secchi/Alamy; p. 112 doglikehorse/Shutterstock;
p. 115 David Sacks/Getty Images; p. 122 View Stock/Getty Images; p. 123 Tim
Gainey/Alamy, 237/Adam Gault/Ocean/Corbis; p. 124 ajafoto/iStockphoto
(chocolate), Stockbyte/Oxford University Press (tomato), Ingram/Oxford
University Press (carrot); p. 126 Lou Veltri/Alamy; p. 127 Paula Solloway/
Alamy; p. 132 Chris Schmauch/Alamy; p. 136 Rudchenko Liliia/Shutterstock;
p. 141 Mikael Karlsson/Alamy; p. 144 Amy Walters/Shutterstock; p. 153
Patrick Forget/AGE Fotostock; p. 154 Izabela Habur/Getty Images (students),
gulfimages/Alamy (businessmen); p. 156 Tom Wang/Shutterstock; p. 163
Serp/Shutterstock; p. 169 Super RF/Alamy (hands), avatra images/Alamy
(board); p. 176 racorn/Shutterstock; p. 182 Richard Herrmann/Minden
Pictures/Newscom; p. 183 Triff/Shutterstock, Ilan Amihai/Alamy, Paul
Biddle/Science Photo Library; p. 184 Doug Allan/Science Photo Library
(iceberg), Andreas Meyer/Shutterstock (space station), Stocktrek Images/
Getty Images (remains), Ocean Image Photography/Shutterstock
(shipwreck); p. 186 Johnny Lye/Shutterstock; p. 188 David J Slater/Alamy;
p. 195 Alaska Stock/Alamy; p. 200 Image Source/Alamy; p. 202 Jeff Rotman/
Getty Images; p. 210 Ernest Doroszuk/ZUMA Press/Newscom, Pakawat
Suwannaket/Shutterstock; p. 211 Blend Images - JGI/Jamie Grill/Getty
Images, David Allan Brandt/Getty Images; p. 212 Juanmonino/iStockphoto
(tennis), Rido/Shutterstock (business clothes); p. 213 Frida Azari/Stuart
Brown MD; p. 214 Hero Images/Corbis UK Ltd.; p. 221 Studio Grand Ouest/
Shutterstock; p. 223 Digital Vision./Getty Images; p. 229 2014
ChinaFotoPress/Getty Images; p. 234 Martin Siepmann/Getty Images.